...to be
continued...

Kabbalah Publishing is a registered DBA of The Kabbalah Centre International, Inc.

For further information:

The Kabbalah Centre
155 E. 48th St., New York, NY 10017
1062 S. Robertson Blvd., Los Angeles, CA 90035

1.800.Kabbalah www.kabbalah.com

First Edition, August 2012

Printed in USA

ISBN: 978-1-57189-862-3

Also available as an eBook ISBN: 978-1-57189-870-8

Design: HL Design (Hyun Min Lee) www.hldesignco.com

...to be continued...

reincarnation
& the purpose of our lives

KABBALAH PUBLISHING

karen berg
spiritual director of the kabbalah centre

Everything came from the seed of Adam.
We all reincarnated from Adam.

(It's funny; today we say it all began with the atom.)

Table of Contents

Preface

If this is the first book you are reading from The Kabbalah Centre, a bit of introduction is in order. Throughout *To Be Continued*, you will read about the Rav. He is my husband, my teacher, and my soul mate. He was given the responsibility of leading The Kabbalah Centre after the passing of his teacher, Rav Brandwein, in 1969. Kabbalah is an ancient spiritual wisdom traditionally reserved for older scholars. But together, the Rav and I opened the doors of Kabbalah to everyone around the world, regardless of age, gender, or religious affiliation, who wished to explore its insights. Though the Rav and I were an unlikely pair—I came from a secular but spiritual background and the Rav from an orthodox one—our unique union became the basis for The Kabbalah Centre you see today: an open forum for those who are as yet uninitiated in the ways of Kabbalah but who have a desire to study Kabbalah and to find a place to do so without judgment or limitation.

At The Kabbalah Centre, we study and apply the teachings of Rav Isaac Luria—also known as the Ari, or the Lion, of Safed—one of the greatest kabbalists who ever lived. He was the author of the 18-volume classic text called *Kitvei HaAri* (*Writings of the Ari*), which interprets, synthesizes, and systematizes the teachings of the *Zohar*, the dense sacred text that is central to Kabbalah. Interestingly, the Ari himself wrote very little of the *Kitvei HaAri*. His oral teachings were captured by his student Rav Chaim Vital, who compiled and transcribed them. In *To Be Continued*, I will be drawing extensively from the Lurianic wisdom, specifically from the volume known as *The Gates of Reincarnation*.

If this is your first contact with us, I welcome you to this discussion of kabbalistic wisdom regarding reincarnation. It is my hope that what you find here will benefit you directly and will inspire you to further study.

Introduction

Is there justice?

A student comes to his teacher and asks, "Tell me, Teacher, is there justice in this world? Or is there only retribution—an eye for an eye and a tooth for a tooth?"

The teacher replies, "Tomorrow, go to the town square and observe what happens there. Then come back and share it with me."

So the next day, the student goes to town and finds a discreet place to watch the goings-on. He sees a man walk over to a bench in the small park at the center of the town square. The man places his large valise under the bench and opens a newspaper. Seeing a friend walking by, however, the man jumps up and joins him, leaving his valise and newspaper behind.

A moment later, another man arrives. He sits on the bench, spots the valise, and opens it, his eyes growing wide as he sees that it's full of money. Quickly looking around and seeing no one, he tips the contents of the valise into his knapsack, kicks the valise back under the bench, and runs off, taking his newly found riches with him.

Now a third man appears and sits on that same bench, leaning back to enjoy the beautiful day. The first man returns and says, "Hey, what did you do with my valise?"

"I didn't see a valise," says the third man.

"What are you talking about? Here it is right under this bench. And its latches are open. What have you done with my money?"

The argument soon turns into a fight. The first man soundly thrashes the unfortunate newcomer, but learns nothing more about his missing money. Finally, exhausted and filled with disgust, he walks away.

That evening, the student goes back to his teacher and recounts what he observed. "So what do you make of this?" the teacher asks. The student says, "From this, I can only conclude that there is no such thing as justice."

"You have eyes, but you do not see!" says his teacher. "In their last lifetime, the first man and the second man were partners in business, and the first man stole a fortune from the second man. Only now is the second man recovering what was taken from him."

"Okay," says the student. "But what about the third man? Why did he get beaten up?"

"When these two partners went to court to settle their differences, the third man was the judge who unjustly sided with the first man."

When we experience this world without an understanding of reincarnation, it often appears to us (as it did to this student) that life is unfair. But this story points out the deeper truth: That although justice might not be immediate or obvious, it will prevail. Karma—the balance between our actions and their consequences, between cause and effect—must be served. We just have to remember that the karmic scales may take a long time to balance out. We may not see that happen in this lifetime or we may see karma from past lives at work today, but either way, we can't truly recognize what's going on without taking reincarnation into account.

If we lived with a full knowledge of reincarnation and karma, we would become keenly aware of the significance of our actions and no longer have that feeling of being victims in a chaotic, whimsical world. Life would make much more sense, and it would be infinitely more fulfilling.

The Soul's Journey

People die, and their bodies decay. But as the first law of thermodynamics tells us, energy can only be transformed; it cannot be created or destroyed. Things don't just disappear in our physical world. Water evaporates, but returns to the earth as rain. Mountains become rocks, which become sand. Even death itself cannot result in a loss of energy, so death isn't really the ultimate end of life.

What's more, the root source of our being—our soul—isn't even part of our physical body. Think of a cup and water. They exist together, but the water is not a part of the cup. If you pour the water out of the cup, the quality and structure of the water doesn't change. The body is also a container, distinct from the soul it houses. So when a person dies, that spark of sacred energy, that is the soul, does not die with that person. It returns to its source, to the Creator. Then, after going through a process of spiritual cleansing, the soul is given the opportunity to find a new container in which to pass another lifetime.

Every soul's journey after death is unique, but almost all souls go through a process of cleansing in a place kabbalists call *Gehenom*. This hell, as the *Zohar* describes it, is not what we commonly take hell to be; it has no fire and brimstone, no devils, pitchforks, or tormented souls. It's not even a fixed location. It's more like a transient laundromat, a place where souls get washed clean—except, that is, for those souls that depart the body on the Sabbath. Because of the special energy of mercy available on the Sabbath, those souls do not go through the same process.

Why does the soul reincarnate again and again? Because it has profound lessons to learn. In one incarnation, a soul may need to learn about being rich; in the next, it may need to learn about being poor. It may need to learn about strength or weakness, anger or compassion, beauty or unsightliness. With each incarnation, the soul returns to the physical world to correct a different aspect of itself. In so doing, the soul gathers sparks of Light back to itself, and the puzzle pieces come together. I'll describe in the next chapter how our lives form a puzzle and how eventually, when the soul is complete, it returns to the source of all Light—the Creator.

Using the concept of reincarnation as a guide, this book will help you discover that your purpose in life from a kabbalistic perspective is to contribute to your soul's journey of discovery. The pages ahead are divided into three parts. In Part I, you will learn about the dynamics of reincarnation—how and why it happens. In Part II, you'll discover why life's challenges are an essential part of your soul's journey. Finally, Part III provides you with practical tools founded in ancient kabbalistic wisdom—including an explanation of angels, kabbalistic astrology, and the traces of past lives that can be found etched in our faces and the palms of our hands—that can help you detect the key patterns in your life. As you become more aware of the inner workings of reincarnation, you can use these tools to discover the reason why you're here in this lifetime. Then, armed with this knowledge, you can devote your energies to helping your soul on the specific journey it must complete before being reunited with the Creator.

Part I

The Puzzle

Chapter 1

Our puzzle

The Creator gives each of us a soul, which I like to compare to a jigsaw puzzle with thousands of pieces. It's our job over many lifetimes to assemble the pieces of this puzzle, to make it whole again. Before we're born into this world—while we're still one with the Creator—we are shown what our particular soul-puzzle looks like with all its pieces in place. Up there, where there are no veils to hide the Creator's truth, we learn that only with a physical body can we continue the work of assembling our puzzle, of completing that part of ourselves that must eventually return to the Creator. We are shown the corrections that remain to be made. This is the work that gives purpose and meaning to our soul's many lifetimes and to this, our latest incarnation.

Once we're born—once our souls are made manifest in this physical world—we can no longer see our soul's pieces in their assembled form. We see only fragments, which we have to blindly fit together ourselves. So we set to work, finding the borders first—our mother, father, siblings, husbands, wives, and children (or the absence thereof). These border pieces fit together to give us the general outline of the puzzle. But then comes the guts of the puzzle, which is far more difficult to assemble because we don't yet know the story that ties all the pieces together. Our mission is to uncover that story.

Sometimes we find a piece that, at first, seems to fit in the right place, but later we discover that maybe it doesn't. But isn't that what happens in life? The seemingly great relationship that doesn't work out? The career we've spent years training for that doesn't make us happy because it just isn't the right fit for us?

So how do we go about putting the puzzle together properly? By first understanding that this work is the reason we are born into this lifetime, and then by being engaged in this process every minute. Life is involvement. We wake up in the morning and embrace the people around us. We nurture business contacts. We savor love-relationships and friendships. There will be people we're not wild about, but still we deal with them. These involvements—some smaller, some greater—are the pieces that make up our lives.

When we see our life as a collection of puzzle pieces, we begin to learn how to handle ourselves in difficult situations. Recently, a friend told me that she went to dinner with someone who said, "Karen Berg? What a terrible person she is." Comments like this continued throughout their dinner. When my friend shared this story with me, I thought, *I could get upset and say "How could he say those things?"* But instead, I realized that this experience, too, is a part of my puzzle. It's just one piece among many. It doesn't have to define me, although I do want to use it to learn something about myself, to see how this piece fits into the bigger picture of my life.

There is a story about King David that sheds light on a similar experience. As King David was travelling, a man named Kasbi cursed him. The king's soldiers moved toward Kasbi to punish him, but King David said, "If he's cursing me, I deserve to be cursed." By this, he meant that if there is something in our life that presents a challenge or a difficulty—like a harsh father, a conniving coworker, a serious illness, or a person who speaks badly about us—this is ours to own (that is, we deserve this) because somehow it fits into the grand plan that our soul came to uncover. There is no such thing as chance: Everything that happens is intended to teach us a lesson or give us a message. Everything.

And if, over many lifetimes, our soul eventually manages to understand all its lessons and puts the entire puzzle back together, then it returns its Light back to where it belongs—with the Creator, the Source of all Light. All of these fragments, these puzzle pieces, will reunite after sufficient lifetimes of working through the challenges we face: This is our purpose for being here on Earth.

Chapter 2

Is reincarnation hocus-pocus?

One thing I'm not here to do is to "build a case" for reincarnation. I prefer to share with you what Kabbalah has to say about reincarnation, knowing that this wisdom can help all of us overcome the hurdles we encounter every day. Indeed, from a kabbalistic point of view, there is no complex argument to be put forward on behalf of reincarnation. Reincarnation is simply a fact of life. End of story.

In the *Gates of Reincarnation*, Rav Isaac Luria (the Ari), describes the many lifetimes of our patriarchs and sages—Adam, Jacob, Esau, Moses, Isaac—and what they came back to learn and correct. We understand from the Ari that he himself was a spark of Rav Shimon bar Yochai, the author of the *Zohar*. In this one volume alone, the Ari explains the deepest mysteries of the soul, including how and why we may reincarnate as animals or even as inanimate objects such as stones.

Despite the kabbalistic belief that reincarnation is a certainty, some people see it as hocus-pocus. But without an appreciation of this process, most of us sleepwalk through life. We wake up, we go to work, we go to school, we come home, eat, watch TV, go to sleep...and do it all over again the next day. Limiting ourselves to information from our five senses keeps us from seeing the deeper meaning in this life at this moment. That's why so many of us feel that life is something that happens to us randomly, bringing joy one day and tragedy the next. Like the student who went to the town square, we don't see how a particular occurrence in this lifetime is connected to events in an earlier one. Once we understand the workings of reincarnation, seemingly random events suddenly take on new meaning.

...to be continued...

Often when we're driving our car while chatting with our passenger, we're surprised when we arrive at our destination. When we don't pay attention, we go on automatic pilot. So it is with other aspects of our life as we follow well-established patterns of thoughts and actions without actually considering what we're doing.

It's always a good idea to carve out new pathways, but this is especially true as we grow older. New thoughts create new connections between neurons in the brain allowing the mind to stay alert, agile, and capable of novel thoughts. Without these new pathways, the brain has a tendency to lose precious functions over time, much like any other organ, muscle, ligament, or bone we don't challenge. The same holds true of the spirit.

Consider the experience of astronauts. How much further from their comfort zones could they get? But by going into the hostile environment of space—by breaking out of their earthly comfort zone—they come back profoundly changed. A kabbalist might say that by going into outer space, astronauts draw from a spiritual source, connecting with the umbilical cord of the Creator's Light. As Above, so Below. Some say that this spiritual cord, which consists of energy, the life-breath of the Creator, allows Light to flow into our world, infusing every atom, molecule, and cell on Earth.

Space is part of that cord. When we travel in space, we connect to the Light and cannot help but come back altered.

Of course, I'm not suggesting you become an astronaut. But I am asking you to reflect on the possibility that reality might be different from what you've been thinking it is. In that spirit, I would like you to try something: Assume for the moment that reincarnation is a fact. This may mean setting aside your more rational mind. The idea here is to let go of what you think you know in order to awaken your consciousness. When you do, I am sure you will see signs all around you supporting this shift.

Near-Death Experiences

People who have gone through a near-death experience often say things like, "I saw people I knew who have already passed over, waiting for me at the other end of the tunnel." They also frequently describe themselves moving toward the light. Most of us don't get the opportunity to experience what it would be like to die and come back to life. People who do, have been given an opportunity to draw from the umbilical cord of Light. Essentially, they're being told by the Creator, "I gave your life back to you because you still have a mission to accomplish."

Most of us have to wait for our next incarnation to continue our spiritual mission, but these rare few who have had a near-death experience have been given a second chance in the same lifetime. A man I know, a healer, once worked as an engineer in a big corporation. He died during a medical procedure, but as he was leaving his body, he heard Heavenly voices saying, "We are going to send you back. But only to help others. You have been given this opportunity in order to use your powers as a healer." Everybody has the power to heal themselves, and perhaps even others, but this man had been given a miraculous gift of healing. He was told, "Now you're going back so you can use it." And he did.

Birthmarks and Birth Defects

Dr. Ian Stevenson, a professor of psychiatry at the University of Virginia, is one of the world's foremost researchers on reincarnation. He traveled extensively from 1966 to 1971 collecting more than 2,600 reported cases of past-life memories, mostly from young children. He published this research in his book *Children Who Remember Previous Lives: A Question of Reincarnation*[1]. Many of these children came from the Buddhist and Hindu countries of South Asia, from the Shiites of Lebanon and Turkey, from the tribes of West Africa, and from the American northwest.

Dr. Stevenson collected specific information from the children's memories and matched it with data from the former identity they claimed—their family, the place where they said they had lived, the manner of their death. He focused on children because they were less capable of making up the many details of a former life. (Or as the Rav would say, they had not yet become ADULT-erated; that is, they were still close to their past-life experiences.) Stevenson believed that particularly violent trauma and death in one life left physical evidence in the next one. He identified more than 40 cases of children and some adults who claimed to have suffered violent deaths in past lives and had birthmarks in the areas of their fatal wounds. Stevenson detailed his research into birthmarks and birth defects in his multi-volume work *Reincarnation and Biology: A Contribution to the Etiology of Birthmarks and Birth Defects*[2].

Stevenson also wrote about Jeffrey Keene's riveting experiences. Keene was an assistant fire chief in Westport, Connecticut. On his 30th birthday, he suddenly experienced severe and worsening pain in his jaw. Several tests were run in the emergency room, but the doctors there couldn't identify the source of the pain. Eventually, it faded. End of story? Not quite.

Some 14 years later, Keene while on vacation, stopped in Sharpsburg, Maryland, the scene of the Civil War battle of Antietam. He felt as if the battlefield called to him. Walking through the "Sunken Road" area, he had a strong emotional and physical reaction, which he describes in his book, *Someone Else's Yesterday: The Confederate General and Connecticut Yankee: A Past Life Revealed*[3].

> *A wave of grief, sadness and anger washed over me. Without warning, I was suddenly being consumed by sensations. Burning tears ran down my cheeks. It became difficult to breathe. I gasped for air as I stood transfixed in the old roadbed. To this day I could not tell you how much time transpired, but as these feelings, this emotional overload passed, I found myself exhausted, as if I had run a marathon....*

Keene did not understand why he had experienced these sensations, but before leaving Sharpsburg, he bought a Civil War magazine that covered the Battle of Antietam. Leafing through the publication many months later, he discovered a picture of General John Gordon, to whom he bore an astonishing resemblance. (The photo on the left compares their facial features.) He learned that the Confederate General was severely injured at Sunken Road on September 17, 1862 during the Battle of Antietam—receiving bullet wounds across his right cheek, on his forehead, and under his left eye. He was 30 years old at the time—the same age that Keene had experienced the mysterious pain in his jaw. Also, Keene has three unique birthmarks in the very same spots that General Gordon had been shot. (You can find photos comparing their faces in the collections of the United States Library of Congress and the National Archives.)

Cases such as Jeffrey Keene's indicate that certain facial features—even when they result from major or even fatal trauma—remain consistent from one lifetime to another. This observation suggests that the soul projects an energy template that shapes the body in general and facial features in particular. I'll have more to say about this in Part III.

Past-Life Memories and Déjà Vu

When we leave this world, the door closes. When we reincarnate, the door reopens. But sometimes when we reincarnate, the door from a past life is left slightly ajar. This explains how some people can remember incidents or specific details from their past lives. When you and I experience such a glimpse, we call this a *déjà vu* experience. In French, these words mean "already seen." You may be sitting with a friend drinking tea, for example, when suddenly you have a strong feeling that you've done this before. Or you may meet someone new and are certain that you already know the person, perhaps very well (don't those hands look incredibly familiar?), but when you consider every conceivable connection, it's clear that no prior meeting could have been possible.

Some *déjà vu* experiences are quite dramatic. Jeffrey Keene, for instance, possessed detailed knowledge of General Gordon's life without ever having read anything about him. Once, while touring a visitor center displaying artifacts of a Confederate surrender ceremony in which General Gordon had participated, Keene noticed a poster depicting the event. Somehow, however, Keene knew that the flag depicted in the print was inaccurate, and he identified the correct one from among a group of flags exhibited at the center. After researching the matter, the staff of the visitor center verified that the flag in the poster was indeed from a later period and that Keene had correctly identified the flag that had actually been used in the ceremony.

There are many reported cases of people who experience past-life memories. Eleven-year-old James Leininger's story was aired on ABC's newsmagazine TV show *Primetime*[4]. The boy knew an extraordinary amount about World War II fighter planes without ever having read about them. He told his parents that he had died in a plane crash, giving them the name of the aircraft carrier he'd been assigned to, as well as the name of his best friend aboard ship. How could he possibly know the names of people he had worked with long before he was born in this lifetime?

His parents, however, were able to validate the historical details he had given them. They discovered that the man their son described had also been named James—James Huston. Eventually, young James's parents reunited their son with James Huston's surviving sister. She came to believe that little James Leininger was indeed the reincarnation of her deceased brother, James Huston, and she gave little James a number of her brother's cherished belongings.

Another fascinating case involved another young girl. Barbro Karlén was born into a devout Catholic family in Sweden. As a small child she was plagued by nightmares of persecution. At the age of 10, she traveled with her family to Amsterdam and felt a powerful impulse to visit the home of Anne Frank. Barbro had not read *Anne Frank: The Diary of a Young Girl*, but when her parents called for a taxi to take them to Anne Frank's home, she told them it wouldn't be necessary because the house was nearby. Much to her parents' surprise, Barbro exhibited a remarkable familiarity with the house and described how things had been moved around. As the family moved on into the hidden rooms,

Barbro became terrified, just as she had been in her dreams. She broke out in a cold sweat and had trouble breathing.

She describes the experience in her novel, *And the Wolves Howled: Fragments of Two Lifetimes*[5], in which she appears as the character Sara.

> *When they went into one of the smaller rooms, she suddenly stood still and brightened up a little. She looked at the wall in front of her. "Look, the pictures of the film stars are still there!"*
>
> *Her mother stared at the blank wall and couldn't understand this at all. "What pictures? The wall is bare." When Sara looked again, she saw that this was true. The wall was bare!*
>
> *Her mother was so confounded that she felt driven to ask one of the guides whether she knew if there had been pictures on the wall at one time. "Oh yes, they had only been taken down temporarily to be mounted under glass so that they wouldn't be destroyed or stolen." Sara's mother didn't know what to say.*

There are many such instances when the door to a past life doesn't quite close completely and we experience *déjà vu*. Why is it that you immediately take a liking to someone you've just met, and within a few minutes, you both feel and act like sisters? The truth is that we have lived before with the people around us, with our friends and family. By the same token, people we instinctively dislike might have hurt us in a prior lifetime, so even though we can't put a finger on exactly why, we feel ill at ease when we're around them and our gut feeling is mistrust.

Where does this come from? Remember that the human body functions through exchanges of electrical energy, positive and negative, and that energy cannot be destroyed or lost; it can only take a new form. What we see and feel in this life can be triggered by experiences from past lifetimes—by people who were around us, who may have cared for or harmed us. This can become quite confusing as we move from one lifetime to another because roles can change. A brother in a past life could have been a father in an even earlier life; a friend could have been a mother, and so on.

Our Fears and Our Past Lives

Another way we can learn about our past lives is through our seemingly irrational fears and phobias. We may be afraid of heights; we may be fearful of water; we may be terrified by snakes or spiders or dogs. Indeed, we may be frightened by all kinds of things that don't seem to make sense in our current life. That's because these fears are the result of what we went through in another lifetime. Perhaps we were mauled by a dog, or we drowned, or we fell to our death while climbing a mountain. By identifying our seemingly inexplicable fears, we can put together more puzzle pieces about our last incarnation.

Our traumatic experiences from past lives correlate with the fears we suffer in this life. People whose previous life ended on 9/11 could be afraid of heights or fire or flying in a plane. Or if we felt love in a past lifetime but each time we gave our heart away we were hurt or perhaps even abused by our spouse, we might be so afraid of love-relationships in this lifetime that we simply refuse to engage in one.

Hypno-Regression

Many people participate in hypno-regression in an attempt to make contact with earlier incarnations. I'm not talking here about a regression in which you are told who you were in a past life, like Queen Elizabeth I or Mata Hari. That's certainly interesting, although I tend to be suspicious that so many of us turned out to have been famous people in past lives. Then again, of course, who would want to pay money to learn they were once a galley slave or a medieval serf or a thief or assassin?

But no, I'm talking here about the soul's journey. We all started out this cycle of reincarnation as sparks of Light, and over the millennia, our soul continues to evolve until we will have entirely restored the rock that we took out of that mountain called the Creator. I'm talking about the process that will eventually allow our completed puzzle to go back into the box from which it came. This process takes untold years—in fact, Light years of incarnations.

The Rav has told me that he and I were together during the Spanish Inquisition. He stayed in Spain and died there, but I converted to Catholicism and left the country. This may well be true, but how do I know for sure? Sometimes I visit psychics and when they corroborate what I know of a past life, I tell myself, Oh well, that must be right. It may not work for you, but for me, a psychic's reading, or hypno-regression, can serve as confirmation. In my opinion, hypno-regression can be a good way to discover things we need to fix in our current lifetime: We can use this information as a tool for change, to find out how we can make a karmic correction, to discover what our mission in life really is.

The Signs Are Everywhere

When you really wish to know if a *déjà vu* moment or a synchronistic event is really a spiritual communication, you can ask the universe to guide you with a sign. I do it all the time. You might pose your question to a random person you don't know; her response will be your answer. Or you can specifically ask to witness an out-of-the ordinary occurrence as confirmation that what you've seen or heard is true: "In four days, let me see two white dogs walking in the street or let two mail trucks in a row pass me by if I'm really meant to take this new job." These kinds of things do happen; they call to you all the time. And if you are aware, if you are fully conscious when they do occur, you'll know you're in the right place.

I have a friend who was in a challenging relationship with a man who lived in Turkey. Dana was in a great deal of pain over it and was trying to decide whether she should go to see him. One day, she went to a local coffee shop and asked for a sign. Moments later as she was about to order her food, her attention was drawn to the sound of people speaking Turkish. She thought, *OMG, This is crazy! This isn't just a sign, its a billboard! Just when I'm deciding whether to go to Turkey, I hear people speaking Turkish in a Belgian boulangerie in NYC!*. Then one of the women said very forcefully in heavily accented English, "She can't fly to Istanbul." That was the only thing they said in English. They then proceeded to continue their conversation in Turkish. My friend was shocked. She went over to the table of people, excused herself for intruding, and asked the woman, "Did you say, 'She *can* fly to Istanbul' or 'She *cannot* fly to Istanbul?'" The woman replied firmly, "She cannot."

Dana had her answer.

Chapter 3

The evolution of the soul

And the spirit returns back to the Creator who gave it.
Namely, it returns back to Him in perfection."

—The *Zohar, Pinchas* 10:48

As I mentioned earlier, various primary sources of Kabbalah, including the *Zohar* and *The Writings of the Ari*, inform us that we are born into this world with a spark of Divine energy and it's our job eventually to return that energy to its original source—the Creator. However, we also need to bring it back "perfected." And if it is not perfected—that is, exactly as it was when it was originally given to us—then it must come back to this physical world in a new vessel to try again.

> *And if the soul does not return perfect as it was WHEN IT WAS GIVEN, the verse says about it, "thither they return," (Ecclesiastes 1:7), it and to all the other souls WHICH ARE LIKE IT, NAMELY NOT PERFECT. IN OTHER WORDS, THEY RETURN TO THIS WORLD IN AN INCARNATION.*

> —The *Zohar, Pinchas* 10:49

What does this mean? Simply that we reincarnate in order to give our soul a chance to mature, to purify, to become perfect. Remember Bill Murray's character in the movie *Groundhog Day*? When the film begins, he's self-centered, narcissistic, and sarcastic, an all-around mean and hurtful person and certainly not someone you'd like to hang out with. His fate is to relive Groundhog Day over and over again. When he discovers this, he gets angry at first and acts out even more. But gradually he comes to understand the value of selfless behavior until he finally gets it right, wins the love of the girl, and is able to move on to the next day—February 3—and a whole new life. We could say that after having to come back again and again, his soul finally evolved to its next phase.

How Does a Soul Evolve?

Over its many lifetimes, the soul changes and develops. Here are the three basic phases of its evolution:

- **Baby phase:** The soul comes down in physical form, eats, sleeps, and plays. It experiences life as if it were a small child.

- **Second phase:** As the soul matures, it looks for more than simple enjoyment. It wants to learn, to develop, to be something more than what it is today.

- **Third phase:** The mature soul realizes it can be fulfilled only through sharing.

The Ari says that the number of times this cycle must be repeated before achieving full correction depends on the individual soul. However, there is a minimum requirement. If a soul goes through its first lifetime with no progress, it is allowed to return three more times. If at the end of that time—that is, after a total of four incarnations—no progress has been made, the soul reverts to the abyss. If, however, progress is made in any of those lifetimes, then no further limit is imposed upon the number of reincarnations needed to complete the mission of correction. But there is a caveat here: Even if progress is made, the danger of plunging backward in any lifetime is always present.

Any soul that has reincarnated more than four times has done part of its work in this world. Over the course of various incarnations, something tells the soul to seek something more than good times. The soul begins to desire a purpose. It may start with a simple feeling: *Hey, I've got to do something for my community*, or *I've got to do something to feed the poor*, or *I need to make sure everyone in the world has clean drinking water.* From this starting point, the soul grows, and as it matures, its energy becomes more refined.

People who help others, their community, or their country may not yet be saying, "I came to this world for a purpose," but they have begun stepping out of themselves and their own individual needs. This can happen at any age and stage of life. When individuals focus on the welfare of others, they become what we call righteous, elevated souls. Indeed, we are all being encouraged by the Creator to ask ourselves, What am I meant to be doing here? But sometimes we need to mature and learn in order to do so. We cannot expect a baby to be motivated by the desire to go to college.

Our Souls Choose Our Destiny

When our soul prepares to reincarnate, we are told what we did in our immediate past life and what work still needs to be finished. We are told what our higher soul needs. At the moment of conception (whether it happens in the traditional way or in vitro), the soul sees the puzzle in its entirety and chooses to take on a particular incarnation, realizing that this is what it needs in order to grow.

But why would a soul choose to be born into overwhelming difficulties, such as disease, abuse, or abject poverty?

While it's still a spark of Light, the soul looks down on this world much like a satellite views the earth. From this vantage point, it can observe not only where it has been, but where it needs to go and what kind of environment will help it finish its correction. The soul identifies the people and circumstances that will help it complete its particular process and then chooses that environment to come into.

The consciousness of the new baby's parents also contributes to the process of determining what type of soul they will attract to themselves. For instance, if a man has sex with another woman and then comes home to sleep with his wife, most likely his thoughts will be somewhere else. Still, he may have sex with his wife out of a sense of duty or guilt. Maybe he's not really into this relationship, or maybe she isn't. Those feelings or lack of feelings—that particular state of consciousness—attracts a soul that needs exactly this setting.

The soul that chooses to be conceived at that particular moment and born to that particular couple will have a corrective process that involves a challenge with parents or relationships. In a former life, this soul may have done something that broke up its family or it may have been a philanderer. To correct that aspect of itself, the soul comes into a home where there is discontent, dissension, or even depression. The soul actually sees this couple's consciousness, recognizes that this difficult relationship will be good for its *tikkun* (the Hebrew word meaning "correction," which is also understood as karma), and chooses to be born into it. The consciousness of the parents helps define the circumstance. The soul may be brought into this particular marriage as a child born "by accident." The couple may have not necessarily wanted a child, but nonetheless, one was conceived. But whatever environment is chosen, it is always the unique soil in which the seed of our soul needs to be nurtured.

Chapter 4

Animals, trees, and stones

Everything around us is constantly engaged in a process of evolution and change. The question for us is this: Do we recognize this evolution when we see it? As the Rav used to say, "Mountains can grow." Even a rock evolves. Hard to believe? Think of it this way. A rock can be ground into cement and that cement can be poured into the foundation of someone's home. The energy that was originally in the rock now provides shelter for the people living in the house, so, in effect, that rock has evolved into something more than its original self. A tree can be cut and formed into a table, sharing its energy with the people who sit around it eating, talking, and laughing. That energy is what allows you to walk into a home and say instinctively, "Oh, it feels so good in here." Or to say to yourself, *This place gives me the willies. I can't wait to get out of here.* What you're sensing is the Light in this table, that chair, this wall—all of which determine the energy in a home.

When a home doesn't feel good, what is it that makes us want to run? Here, too, a rock was ground up into cement and poured into the foundation, and a tree was fashioned into a table or chair. The discomfort we're feeling comes from the specific energy of that particular piece of wood or rock, together with how it was used and who used it.

The truth is, everything has energy and energy can never be destroyed. A spark of Light resides within every single bit of matter in the universe. Adam was the original complete spark of Light that came from the Creator. He was tasked with implanting the Light in all of creation. By naming the animals, he imbued them with sparks of that Light energy. He said,

"Horse," and a spark entered the horse. The *nitzot*, or sparks of Light, that Adam placed in everything marked the beginning of evolution.

The energy or spark in an animal or a stone originally came from man and can return to man. Part of our job in this physical world is to elevate these non-human, non-animate sparks each time we interact with them. When we use objects—whether a dress, a piece of cake, or a bench—with the consciousness of doing so for the sake of revealing Light, we actually elevate the spark within those objects.

This reminds me of something that happened at The Kabbalah Centre. A well-meaning person inadvertently sold the wooden benches in the sanctuary. This greatly upset the Rav because of the amount of energy in those benches, which over the years had been imbued with the essence of the people who sat on them and engaged in study and discussion and prayer. The benches were so important that we tracked them down and brought them back to The Centre. We wanted and needed their positive energy around us.

Reincarnating into Non-Human Forms

Why did I begin this chapter with a discussion of energy and its presence in inanimate objects like tables, benches, and cement walls? Kabbalah teaches that when our soul returns to this earth without mending its ways, it can come back in a variety of different forms. According to the Ari, our souls can reincarnate as animals, plants, and even inanimate objects. The spark of Light in a leaf or a rock can become a human soul—or vice versa—as part of the spiritual evolutionary process.

Why does this happen? Because we need to experience something in that incarnation—through the experience of being a rock, a leaf, or a pet—that we couldn't learn any other way. Life is meant to be lived with all its challenges. Many people try to duck out on life by turning to drugs or alcohol. I do understand that addiction is a sickness, but from a spiritual perspective, people who self-medicate are, in essence, choosing not to play the game anymore. But no one else can play our personal game for us. When we check out and don't take responsibility for the life our soul has chosen, we may have to reincarnate in non-human form to learn to appreciate both our ability to choose and the importance of our choices.

Sometimes we can look into the eyes of a person who is heavily stoned and say, "There's no one there." When a person takes heavy drugs, his or her body can become an empty vessel; no consciousness occupies it. But from a kabbalistic perspective, we know that an empty body creates an opportunity for something else to enter us, God forbid. Indeed, such a person can attract a *dybbuk*, a malevolent spirit. We will consider dybbuks later on.

It's a Dog's Life

What do we have that animals don't? We have the ability to understand spiritual laws and to decide whether or not we will follow them. We have the ability to play the game or to duck out. We have the ability to say no. And the decisions we make in this life will help determine what form we take in our next one.

Many domesticated animals have human souls that missed opportunities in earlier incarnations. Now, in their non-human vessels, they are learning the importance of choice and restriction.

What is restriction? Every time we receive energy for ourselves alone, we are being controlled by our Desire to Receive. Every time we greedily grab energy without sharing—whether said energy is in the form of sex, money, drugs, alcohol, or success—when we just take without giving something in return, we partake of what kabbalists call Bread of Shame. Yes, we will receive the energy, and it will fill us up for a second, creating the rush we crave—but only in the short run. Then it will short-circuit, and instead of joy, we will find shame, negativity, and chaos in our lives. When we practice restriction, on the other hand, we consciously choose not to act in ways that lead to Bread of Shame.

A human soul that has reincarnated as a dog has lost the opportunity to practice restriction because it didn't practice restriction in its last lifetime as a human. That person became greedy and self-involved, taking energy without giving anything back. And now that soul has been returned to the physical dimension to learn about restriction as a dog, which can do nothing but learn through observing how other people give back and what happens if they don't.

Imagine this scenario. An alcoholic man dies of cirrhosis of the liver because he refused to take himself by the hand and stop drinking. Now he has reincarnated in the body of a dog that has to watch helplessly as his alcoholic master destroys his life. The dog is pained by the situation, but he's an animal and can't talk so there's nothing he can do to help but be there. This is how a spiritual teacher feels when he sees a student going down the wrong road. You can't say, "Don't go there," because people need to learn these lessons for themselves. But not being able to do more to help is very painful.

As for the soul in the dog who observes his master's self-destruction, it can now see what it did to itself in its last life. But there's nothing the soul can do about it. Yet, after the dog dies, however, the soul eventually returns to this world in human form once more and is given another chance. But without that understanding, gained as a dog, of what it came to correct. Learning about our past lives and what we came to correct is essential to enable us to do the work of this lifetime.

Imagine another scenario in which a man had been a drug dealer. He'd hurt a lot of people in his last lifetime, not because he wanted to but because he needed money for his own habit. He peddled cocaine to teenagers and killed a couple of rivals in a turf war along the way. Now he has reincarnated as a cat whose owner is a social worker, devoted to working with troubled teenagers so they can resist peer pressure to turn to crime for money, power, and prestige. The cat's soul observes this and thinks, *Why didn't I see this when I was a human? Why weren't my eyes open to choosing this kind of life?* Fully aware of what it did in its former life, this soul will have to wait for another incarnation to begin changing the effects of its past actions. For now, it can only watch.

The Ari's Goat

As we've seen, all sparks of Light, all souls, evolve through a process of cleansing. Yet occasionally, we find an exception. There is a story in the *Zohar* about Rav Pinchas ben Yair's donkey, whose soul turns out to be the same as that of the donkey of Bilaam. So here we have a case of a donkey that did not evolve over a long period of time. Why? Because this donkey was really more like an angel. The donkey could speak, for one thing, and would eat only if his owners tithed from the grain they fed him.

More typical is the story of a goat that came to the Ari and said, "It's my time. I cannot live in this body any more." The soul trapped in the goat was now ready to reincarnate back into a human being. But the goat told the Ari, who could understand the language of animals, "I need to be killed properly so my soul can elevate. My body must be consumed. That's the only way can I go to my next level." So the Ari obliged the goat by giving it a kosher slaughter. This process is painless and mercifully swift. Also, according to the Bible, the soul resides in an animal's blood, and in the koshering process, all the blood is drained so that no aspects of the soul remain in the body. Once this process was complete, the Ari then prepared and ate the goat, enabling the human soul within the animal to elevate to human form.

In some rare cases, the souls of very evil people reincarnate into animals. By eating a piece of meat from an animal that was inhabited by an evil soul, we can become host to a *dybbuk*, as the soul of that negative person jumps into our being. By draining an animal's blood, we ensure that no negative spirit remains in the animal. This is one of the spiritual benefits of eating kosher meat.

There is a positive side to reincarnating as an animal. We know that the soul of a righteous person who has only a small correction left to make in this world will often enter into the body of a fish. The *Zohar* tells us that the fish we eat on the eve of the Sabbath is imbued with the spark of a righteous person. This helps us elevate our own consciousness on Sabbath, allowing us to receive even greater energy.

Turning to Stone

One of the corrections for people who use a lot of negative speech, who seem to enjoy wounding others with their words, is to be reincarnated as a rock. This is like an indefinite prison sentence, a form of purgatory in which the person can remain for however long.

The Ari finds this correction at work in the story of Bilaam the sorcerer, which can be found toward the end of the biblical *Book of Numbers*. The Ari explains that the soul of Bilaam had four incarnations. First, it incarnated as Laban HaArami, Jacob's father-in-law and a very negative person. Its next incarnation was as Bilaam, the prophet who had the power to cast curses on people. After that lifetime, Bilaam's soul was reincarnated as a rock because Bilaam had used his mouth negatively, and as a stone, he could no longer do so. Bilaam's soul had a fourth incarnation as Nabal HaKarmeli, a man who is also the subject of an interesting story in I Samuel 25.

King David, before he had been anointed king, sent a group of his men to a prosperous man named Nabal HaKarmeli, instructing them as follows: "Tell Nabal that when his people were traveling with their herds, my warriors protected him. In return for this protection, I now ask that Nabal give my people food and drink so they can sustain themselves."

The Ari says there were many other people King David could have turned to for food and drink, but he chose to send his messengers to Nabal. And what did Nabal say? Although he knew King David full well, Nabal replied, "Who is David? There is no way I'm going to help this nobody."

Abigail, the wife of Nabal, overheard this conversation and realized that her husband had made a terrible mistake. Without telling Nabal, she ran after the messengers, stopped them, and gave them food and drink. But she was too late to save her husband from a fatal heart attack. According to the words of I Samuel 25:37: "His heart died within him and he became like a rock."

It looks as if Nabal wasted that incarnation. After all, he did something terrible at the end of his life and died because of it.

But the Ari gives us a deeper insight into the spiritual process at work here. King David was not simply sending messengers to some random person. He knew that Bilaam's soul had reincarnated in Nabal, so he sent his messengers there in order to give Bilaam/Nabal a chance at spiritual correction. Unfortunately, Nabal was still unable to hold his tongue.

But what happened next? The Ari says that suddenly everything was revealed to Nabal. He realized that he was the incarnation of Laban and Bilaam, and that because he had used his mouth negatively as Bilaam, he had been reincarnated into a stone. Now he saw that he had missed this second chance provided by King David. So upset did Nabal become over his latest failure that he had a heart attack and died.

When we read the story literally, it seems that Nabal was not a very good person. But if we step back, we come to appreciate the extraordinary measures he took to elevate his soul. The Ari tells us there was greatness in the soul of Laban/Bilaam/the stone/Nabal. The Ari reveals that Nabal's death was *moteh sharim* (the death of righteousness). Indeed, because Nabal became aware of all his incarnations and felt so keenly the pain of missing an opportunity for elevation, he achieved something extraordinary: Nabal corrected all his lifetimes with this one death.

The lesson here is that no matter how negative we are, no matter how far we fall, there is still a way back—even if we must reincarnate as a rock. Our soul always has an opportunity to reincarnate and correct.

A Reincarnation Timetable

There are four grades of incarnation, which can take hundreds or thousands of years to accomplish: Rock, plant (leaf), animal, human. When a human soul is locked into one of the lower levels, it doesn't always have the strength to elevate and be corrected. Fortunately, there are certain windows of time in which the soul is given a special opportunity to rise. This is the meaning of the oft-quoted biblical phrase: "To everything there is a season and a time to every purpose under heaven." (Ecclesiastes 3:1)

When a human soul reincarnates into an inanimate object, it is sentenced to a certain number of years in that state. When it is time for it to ascend from inanimate object to plant, it can do so only during the Hebrew months of *Av, Elul, Tishrei,* and *Cheshvan.* Otherwise, it has to wait until those months recur in the following year. Ascending from plant to animal occurs during the months of *Nissan, Iyar, Sivan,* and *Tammuz,* and from animal to human in the months of *Kislev, Tevet, Shevat,* and *Adar.* However, a soul residing in an animal can jump these steps by being ritually killed and eaten like the Ari's goat.

Iburs

An *ibur* is a positive spirit, the soul of a righteous person that comes to our aid by entering our being when we are in need. An *ibur* can come from merit we have earned.

In The *Gates of Reincarnation,* the Ari tells his student and scribe, Chaim Vital, that Vital's wife is not his soul mate, and that, in fact, her soul is male. When a male soul exists in a woman, she cannot bear children, so in order to have a child, Rav Chaim Vital's wife needs the assistance of an *ibur.* This *ibur* (who is the soul of Rachel, the wife of Rabbi Akiva) enters the wife of Chaim Vital, who gives birth to a baby girl. The *ibur* then enters the baby, but the infant dies. So once again the *ibur* of Rachel's soul attaches to the wife of Chaim Vital. She becomes pregnant again, and again she bears a daughter. The soul of Rachel enters this child, too, and this time the girl lives.

Dybbuks

As mentioned previously, malicious entities that can enter our being are called *dybbuks.* These are the displaced souls of dead people who turned away from the Light voluntarily or were denied the Light because of serious transgressions. They were unable to fulfill their *tikkun* during past lifetimes so they are being given another opportunity to do so.

The word *dybbuk* comes from a Hebrew word meaning "attachment." If we have created an opening by a loss of consciousness or a negative act, we can become inhabited by a *dybbuk.* We can also contract one innocently by drinking from a stream or river. If a negative spirit dwells in a river and we drink from its waters directly without a cup, we can absorb this negative spirit. It can enter our bodies, and suddenly we will find ourselves behaving in a different way. This is the reason for the spiritual precept not to drink directly from a stream, but to always use a vessel of some kind.

Part II

The Pieces

Chapter 5

Our challenges

Vayehi erev, vayehi boker, yom echad. (Genesis 1:5)

From darkness comes Light.

Everything that happens in our lives, whether good or bad, is a piece of our puzzle. And everything that happens contains lessons. The people and experiences that greet our soul after we come into this world—from the parents who try to shape us in their image, to the person sitting next to us at work; from the friend who betrays us, to the teacher who believes in us—all these have been with us before. We are part of a circle that continues to form our environment from one lifetime to the next... until we make the appropriate corrections. Once we are aware that this is the situation, we can and should also understand that: "If my boss fires me or my girlfriend breaks up with me, then there is something I need to learn from this; there may be something I need to do better, or perhaps the situation itself is just making me a better person. One thing is for sure—it has come to help me."

At The Kabbalah Centre, we teach this point over and over again because in many ways, it is counterintuitive. Light doesn't come through Light. Light comes through darkness. Light is revealed through our difficulties, our pain. When something negative happens, it doesn't mean we are being punished. Kabbalah tells us that there are no victims. *It's through our challenges that we perfect our souls and become who we need to be.*

And the more elevated we become, the greater our challenges become, too.

Light and Dark

The *Zohar* says:

> *The secret of reincarnation is that Light can come out of darkness. Darkness comes out of Light, Abraham who came out of darkness, Terach. Darkness before Light like Eisav who came first.*

—The *Zohar*, Behar 11:64

We are put on this Earth for three reasons:

1. **Love:** To love ourselves, others, and God.

2. **Forgiveness:** To learn how to forgive. There is no such thing as a body without Light. We should be great enough to love the worst of human beings the way the Creator loves the worst of human beings.

3. **Transformation:** Our ability to feel pain is a good thing. In fact, it is one of the most important tools the body gives us. Our challenges provide us with opportunities to move from one level to another, for Light and dark are parallel and of equal measure. The greater the darkness that is overcome, the greater the Light that will be revealed.

Imagine being the child of an abusive father, born into a life with all of the difficulties that a beginning like that can bestow. But such a childhood could also help make you into the best and most compassionate person you can be. What you have gone through may allow you to see in others the spark that they cannot see in themselves. Yes, this is very hard to do, and no one is saying it's not. But it can be done. People free themselves from the most tenacious addictions. It's certainly possible. Yes, sometimes it might feel as if you're fighting with one hand tied behind your back, but remember that we're all moving from the darkness into the Light.

The Paradoxes of Good and Bad

Sometimes what seems good can actually be bad for us— because it may be a block that keeps something better from coming in its place. Consider a relationship that is too comfortable to end, despite the fact that it is no longer right for you. Even the closeness between a mother and her son can be harmful if the son feels so safe and comfortable with his mother that he decides not to create the space to find his mate.

Some people think that having a lot of money is very important. "People who are rich really have it made," we hear them say. But wealth and power don't necessarily make for virtuous or happy people, and they even have a downside we may not have considered. People (men in particular) who are really, really rich are faced with constant temptations, which may lead them to be philanderers. The power that comes with great wealth can make it more difficult for men to be satisfied spending time at home and their marriages, wives, and children can all suffer for it. There is a hidden price for wealth.

Consider, too, the role of money when it comes to beating an addiction. An addict has to acknowledge that he is an addict before he can begin to fight the addiction. How does he do that? Alcoholics Anonymous says: "A person has to feel as if he/she has lost everything, and by so doing, he'll come back." But sometimes a person has so much money that he can't really hit rock bottom. His wealth can buy whatever he wants, and unfortunately that includes all the drugs he needs to eventually kill himself. In this situation, wealth is a curse, not a blessing.

Life is a grab bag of inconsistency and paradox. A person can be fabulously wealthy and still feel less secure or fulfilled than if he had to pick through dumpsters to survive. At The Kabbalah Centre, we call our prayer book *Tefila LeAni,* or *Prayer of the Poor,* to remind us that in this physical world, we're all spiritually impoverished, regardless of what our bank statements may say. We are all empty vessels seeking Light. We come into this world, which has no Light of its own, to draw down Light through our own actions. As it is said, "Who is a rich man? He who is satisfied with what he has."

Poverty and wealth are just two sides of the same coin; both are extreme states that can provide us with what we need to grow spiritually. Many years ago, the Rav and his teacher, Rav Brandwein, paid a visit to a man who was sick with cancer. The man was complaining, "How can God do this to me? I am a good person. I'm observant. I pray and follow all the precepts. How can this be?" When they left, Rav Brandwein said to the Rav that it was a shame this man was missing his opportunity.

In this man's case, as a member of a religious community, the man had been born into spiritual wealth. His illness was his opportunity to show who he was to his Creator, to show that he knew this cancer was what he needed to help him connect to the Light. Instead, he felt like a victim—as if God had punished him undeservedly. Had he truly understood, he would have known that his illness was a part of his *tikkun*, his karma, and therefore vital to the elevation of his soul. It is not what happens to us but how we deal with it that determines our connection to the Creator.

I once heard a revealing adage: "What is the difference between religion and spirituality? Religious people are afraid of going to hell. Spiritual people have already been there." People who become involved in spirituality usually get there through the school of hard knocks, which has forced them to choose between victim-consciousness and the path of growth. They may have had to turn their pain into something positive by saying to themselves, *Okay, all these bad things happened in my life. What can I do with this? How do I use this for good? How can I make meaning of it?*

Now let's look at this issue of good and bad from another angle. I was visiting a student who was serving time at a correctional facility when he asked, "Why is it that with so many people praying for me, I still wind up in prison?" And the answer we came to together was this: Had he not been locked up, he would probably be dead today due to his drug and alcohol addictions. Prison saved his life. So who are we to say his incarceration was a bad thing?

Another young man, Angel, was part of a program we conducted in Panama at the *Rehabilitation Centre El Renacer* prison. Angel could have easily taken the "woe is me" route, but instead he chose to share.

This is a letter he sent me from Panama:

My name is Angel Francisco Lopez and I've been in jail for 32 months. I started to study Kabbalah three months after my admission to prison. At the beginning, the impotence of being in a situation like mine—one I never thought possible because I've always being a good person involved in culture who achieved certain level of fame in the music industry of Spain—made me feel an absolute sadness and depression. I was seeing myself as a victim of a malevolent plan to accuse me and my wife of criminal activity and to keep us locked in prison.

Thanks to the courses that The Kabbalah Centre volunteers give weekly in El Renacer, I was able to learn the amazing tools that this knowledge gives. I realized that I was here for an important reason; I left aside my victim feelings. Little by little, I was able to get out of my depression and sadness, and I began to realize that I am not an island. I started to identify my own limitations; to fight my ego, which is the root of every problem; to share selflessly; and to take advantage of my time and stop complaining to myself.

When I arrived to this Rehabilitation Centre, I found out that there was a modest music studio, but there was no one capable to take care of it. Immediately I got involved. Little by little, I started to apply what I learned from Kabbalah, and everything began to flow. I realized that through my knowledge in music, I could help my fellow-inmates find a way of expressing themselves. I guided them to develop lyrics that give value to society, to create change in the people who have passed through here and many who are already free.

I experienced cases of young adults who felt proud of themselves for being able to create music with a message. They realized that they could aspire to something positive in their lives. Many of them maintain their musical careers still today. Little by little, I got donations from private institutions to improve the conditions of the studio so that we could create and produce our own music. My intention with the remodeling was to share, to transmit. With the help of interns, I've produced more than 60 songs.

Last year I had the idea of writing a theme for peace from prison. I wanted to teach society that not everything here is dark and evil. I'm convinced that the Light, how we call God in Kabbalah, used me as a channel to convey an

... **to be continued** ...

important message to the Panamanian society, first with a theme that was recorded with the prisoners who were working in the project. Later, the theme generated the interest of a cultural center. They helped us contact some local artists to record a second version with more voices involved. When the theme was finished, it was presented in an event in the Rehabilitation Centre El Renacer.

The minister attended. We talked to him for awhile, and he visited the studio, taking with him a CD with the song. A few days later, he told me that he loved the theme and wanted to know if I was interested in recording it again, but this time in a good studio and with known artists! The seed that we planted one afternoon with my friends when I told them about writing a song for peace that will reach everywhere became a reality. I had the total support of the director of the Centre and penitentiary system to record the song for peace. It was chosen as the anthem of the Annual Concert for Peace that was held on April 17, 2011.

All this would have been impossible if my attitude had not been oriented by the knowledge acquired by Kabbalah. Today I trust the Light 100 percent. I know that my time here was provided by the Creator and that my future will be filled with the fruits of the different seeds that I plant day to day. I know that my personal work has to be on a daily basis and that my artistic gifts have a role to transmit this knowledge because it is needed today more than ever for the future of humanity.

There Are No Victims Here

Imagine a beautiful woman for whom appearance is everything. Her clothing, her makeup, her hair, her shoes, the way she acts, her home, her family, the table she sets: Everything must be just so. We probably all know someone like this. And then she gives birth to an imperfect baby. Why does something like this happen? Did the Creator make a mistake? Of course not. Perhaps the lesson she needs to learn is that life is imperfect.

We usually don't like to think of the problems we encounter in our lives as *ours*. We want to blame someone or something else for misfortune: Our parents, our husband, our kids, our boss, God, the weather, the government. We think this way because it's difficult to see ourselves as we really are. We don't want to understand what the puzzle pieces mean in our lives.

But if we believe the spark of God is in all of us, then we can never be victims. We take responsibility for making the only real choice this life offers us: Growth or no growth. Playing the role of victim implies that there is no Light. Playing the role of victim denies the very existence of God's spark.

If a woman allows her husband to abuse her, it's because she doesn't realize that she can become something different. Rather than blaming her husband (or herself), what if she looked at the abuse as a lesson for the growth of her soul? The truth is that she is being invited to recognize the Light in herself and respect it—and to decide not to allow her husband to abuse it any longer. I know this sounds far more simplistic than it is. And I know that no two abusive circumstances are the same. Each presents its own choices and challenges. But healing begins with awareness of the Light within.

The question I often get asked is: "If a person is abused in this life, does this mean that they were an abuser in a past life?" Frequently the answer to this question is yes, but we don't need reincarnation to see that. Research shows that an abused child will very often become an abusive adult.

Let me say emphatically, however, that this does not mean you have to stand there and take the abuse. Ongoing pain is not something you deserve. But it helps to understand that abused people may have been abusers in their past lives and that they may need to feel the same pain themselves in order to restore the spark of Light they took away from another with their previous hurtful actions. We need to understand that the system is perfect, that the universe would not allow us to be hurt for no reason. Knowing this, we can take steps to stop the abuse of the Light that each of us carries within.

Often souls are born into circumstances that are just the opposite of those they left behind. A soul that was disfigured in the last life might come into this one physically beautiful. As we've seen, a soul that was very rich in the last life can come into this life very poor. The soul is given the opportunity to grow in a variety of ways, to taste contrasting aspects of life. But regardless of the kind of life we come into, it's our response to challenges that will ultimately determine the number of lifetimes it takes for our soul to "get it" and return to the Light.

Pick Your Battles/Choose Your Challenges

Some challenges seem to be thrust upon us, but some we bring upon ourselves. To grow, we need to understand that we can sometimes make mountains out of what are really molehills. As we face our trials and tribulations, we need to decide whether we are dealing with *boulders*—those major life-changing events—or *pebbles*—those minor annoyances that seem important but really aren't. Indeed, when we look at the issue carefully, we realize that most of life's problems are not worth the energy we devote to them.

For instance, I know people whose children are healthy, productive, and happily doing their thing. Yet these parents get angry at their kids because they're not behaving the way the parents want them to. They're not living up to expectations. They forget to bring their knapsacks home from school; they don't call on a birthday; they don't bring the grandkids by often enough.

These parents need to ask themselves, *What do I want? My children are decent, kind, generous people. They're not on drugs; they're not thieves; they're living good lives. So what, they didn't call last Sunday. So what, they went to their in-laws instead of coming to our house.* We all tend to get upset by petty grievances, but it's useful to see that they're just molehills. We might even ask ourselves, *Are our children there for us when we need them? Do they call regularly even if they didn't this time?* Who knows? Maybe this time, God forbid, something out of the ordinary happened that got in the way.

Any problem can become a mountain if we make it so. But if we say to ourselves, *Are the kids not what we want them to be? That's okay. Sure, they could be more. But we could be more, too,* then we can put our issues into a healthier perspective.

Women come to me and say, "You know, I love my husband, but he's not amorous enough for me," or "He doesn't enjoy theater and museums," or "He doesn't bring me fancy gifts and flowers on our anniversary." To them I say, "You've got a man who loves you. You've got a man who is generous with you. You've got a man who is there for you. You want more? Take a good look at yourself. Are *you* everything *you* should be? Are you giving everything you would like to receive?"

Unfortunately, a lot of us screw up our lives really badly because of molehills, pebbles, and other nonsense. We create problems where none existed.

Why Do Children Suffer?

If God is all-knowing and all-powerful, how does God make a mistake? Why do we sometimes feel there is no justice in this world? Did we misjudge God's words? For instance, when we see a child who is born into this world mentally challenged or suffering from cerebral palsy, cancer, cystic fibrosis, muscular dystrophy, or any of those terrible disorders that can make life so hard, we rail at God and think to ourselves, *That's not fair!* And we ask ourselves, *If the Creator is good and all His works are good, why do children suffer?*

But let's step back for a moment and consider this situation another way. Imagine, for instance, that while driving and texting, a person runs over and kills a child. The parents of that child might ask the very same question about justice that we asked. But the answer, according to Rav Isaac Luria, is that God didn't create the situation. It wasn't God Who was behind the wheel of that car. It wasn't God Who was too busy with a smartphone to pay attention to what was happening around Him. It wasn't God Who killed the child. It was the driver who hadn't overcome his self-absorbed nature in this lifetime. He's the one responsible for the pain and destruction caused by his actions.

So when this distracted driver eventually dies and prepares for his next reincarnation, his soul is shown its personal puzzle and is given a choice: "If you come back as a wounded or damaged person, you can restore that part of the Light you removed when you killed the child." His suffering through the deformity of his body in his new life recaptures the bit of spark he had lost in his past life and elevates his soul. When we understand that death is not the end, but simply an opportunity to enact a different role, to live through different sides of an experience, it makes our mistakes feel less irreparable and our hardships more tolerable.

A person kills a child. According to the universal plan, this child was intended to die at that moment. Perhaps she needed another incarnation in order to complete an aspect of her spiritual work. So the death is not in question. What is in question, however, is why her death had to come at the hand of this distracted driver? There was a debt to be repaid, an imbalance to be redressed. The individual who killed the child may well come back in the next lifetime with some kind of deformity or unusual burden. He will learn his lessons, feel pain, pay off the spiritual debt, and then reincarnate again, but this time in a healthier state.

Our lack of understanding of the bigger picture makes our actions, our failures, and our mistakes feel fatal and irrevocable. But they are not. They are just pieces of the puzzle. In fact, as we've seen, the only way the soul can make a correction is by coming back in a body that suffers. That's why so many souls come back into these painful situations: It's a way for them to elevate a spark of Light they had lost or diminished. There may be lessons for the parents in this as well, but usually when a child is born with a disability, it's because that soul is being given an opportunity to undo some damage it had caused in an earlier lifetime.

Indeed, this is the only real way to make amends. Going to jail for texting while driving is neither a just nor an adequate price to pay for destroying a life. The only true restoration of balance comes through reincarnation. And a child's death is part of that larger process. It has nothing to do with the Creator. The Creator is unconditionally good.

Think about the untouchables in India. "Untouchable" people are born into a caste system that classifies them as impure, as less than human. Or consider how in some societies, if a child is born of an adulterous relationship, then he is marked for the rest of his life as being a bastard. How could a loving God allow an innocent child to be so tainted from birth?

Again, the answer may lie several lifetimes back. Let's assume for a moment that this newborn baby has taken on the soul of a man who committed adultery two generations before. Now this soul is reborn, but still it must bear the weight of what happened in an earlier lifetime. This isn't simply an innocent baby being born. There is a soul in that infant vessel that needs to correct in a specific way.

Perhaps this perspective gives us a way to understand something that often doesn't make much sense to us. The Bible talks about punishing the iniquity of one generation on the next. To us, this sounds like punishing innocent children. But it really refers to the lifetimes we are given to come back, to make amends, and to elevate the Light of our soul.

Balancing Our Tikkun Process over Lifetimes

As a young man, Avram, a printer's assistant, worked with the great kabbalist Rav Yehuda Ashlag. Avram was born with a deformity on his hand that saddened him because he believed that no woman would want to marry him because of this flaw. But Rav Ashlag explained to Avram that in a former life, he had been one of the spies who spoke badly to Moses about the land of Israel and that the deformed hand was his payment. "You should be happy about this deformity," Rav Ashlag explained, "because it is giving you the opportunity to cleanse your soul."

Once he understood this, Avram was happy. He married and lived a full and productive life. Without that understanding, however, he might have become embittered and pushed away his soul mate or acted out in ways that would have brought him greater difficulties. It is the bigger picture—that our soul lives through many lifetimes—that many of us miss. Explaining the truth about reincarnation is one thing I can do to help you to appreciate this bigger picture as well as all the happiness that comes with it.

Our Spiritual Bank Account

Another question I've been asked a lot recently is why there is so much negativity in the world. The answer: Because people are negative. The carpet we've been comfortably sweeping things under for years is now being picked up and beaten, and all that dust is flying out. People who have taken things that didn't belong to them are being exposed, including bankers who lined their own pockets by creating dangerously risky investments and people who bought houses they couldn't afford without any thought about the future.

Now "all of a sudden" (or so it seems to us), we have to pay the piper. "Wait," we say, "I don't have the money to pay the piper." So the house goes back to the bank. But that's not because there's something wrong with the Light. No, indeed. It's because there's something wrong with us: We took things that didn't belong to us. We knew we shouldn't have, but we took them anyway because we were tempted by greed and covetousness.

All of us have personal accounts in the Bank of Light, which consist of all the positive things we've done. We're constantly drawing from that account. We draw our health. We draw the fact that our mind is in the right place. We draw the fact that our friends and loved ones are healthy and safe. We're constantly withdrawing from that account. But if we take out more than we put in, we're headed for bankruptcy or default, just as with a physical bank account. And that's what is currently happening in the world today. The world is upside down precisely because for years we have been taking more than we have given. But it's not God Who created this upside-down world, and while we can blame the powers that be—Wall Street, the banks, our government—the problem is not with them. The fault lies with *us*.

If we didn't have so much greed, we wouldn't have so much pollution and we'd be able to breathe fresh air. If we didn't destroy our fields, we'd be able to grow healthy food in them. So whose fault is it? God's fault, right? No, it's not! It's my fault, it's your fault, it's everybody's fault. We created the negativity in the first place. We have to look inside ourselves and say, "If we hadn't fouled the water, we'd be able to drink it."

Like It or Not, We Face Our Challenges Alone

No one else can overcome your challenges. No one else can pull you out of the hole you may find yourself in. Why? Because your challenges are specially tailored to your own *tikkun*, your own correction process. It would be like asking somebody else to play your tennis game for you, like giving your friend the racquet and saying, "Here, you hit the ball." It doesn't work like that.

We are all playing a game, and it's called the game of life. What do I mean by that? It's a serious game of return-the-Light-to-where-it-came-from. Hit the ball to the Creator, please.

Chapter 6

Parents and children; children and parents

Children have no veils between themselves and the Light; they're still connected to the Light while they're growing up. However, at 12 years of age for a girl and 13 for a boy, children become ADULT-erated. They lose their direct connection to the Light. Now, for better or worse, they're on their own.

Before they reach this age, children operate on Alpha level all the time. Alpha is the state between wakefulness and sleep that we adults can reach only through meditation. This is why children have sharper instincts than we do. Animals also function at Alpha level, which is why you should pay attention if someone approaches you, and your kids or pets back away. Chances are good that something's wrong with this person's energy. If your dog becomes so upset that the fur on his neck stands up, be very careful of this individual. These Alpha reactions indicate that something is amiss.

When we bring a child into this world, it means that we have been an initiator for an entity of Light. But it's not *our* Light; it is the child's Light. Many parents, however, want to bind their children to themselves. They want their kids not to make a move without consulting them, to get their parental okay for everything they do. But we need to let our children live their lives—because it's their spark, not ours. We are just initiators. They are pieces in our puzzles, it's true, but they also have puzzles of their own.

...to be continued...

Switching Roles

Sometimes when we grow up, we feel we have to take care of our parents. This kind of role reversal can happen because in earlier incarnations, our mother may have been our daughter, or our father a son. To be clear, the role of a mother is exclusively to bring down a soul, a spark of Light, and to enable it to grow into the life it's meant to lead, which includes correcting the karma it brought with it from a past life. The mother's womb is like a cradle. In kabbalistic terms, we would say that it nourishes the vessel that houses the spark of the soul, encouraging it to develop as it will, for negative or positive. The spiritual precept to respect one's mother and father is an acknowledgment of this responsibility.

As important as it is to respect our mothers and fathers, we must also acknowledge the importance of our spiritual teachers, for they nourish our spiritual vessel and encourage its growth. Our teachers are the parents of our souls. One could argue that if someone has mentored you, helping you become the spiritual person you are today, your respect for that person should be even greater than your respect for your parents. This is not to say that we should be disrespectful to our parents. But let's say your father says to you, "Come on! Let's go out and get some beers together," and your teacher says, "Why don't we study?" you can be very nice to your Dad, but you should listen to your teacher.

Chapter 7

Love and soul mates

At the turn of the last century in a village in Eastern Europe, there was a small temple whose rabbi was aging. Simon, the town's mayor and its wealthiest citizen, sent out inquiries to the most famous *yeshivas* (religious seminaries) in Europe, hoping to recruit the services of a young man to assume the duties of the failing rabbi. Many candidates replied, and several were invited for an interview. One of these men had the most remarkable presence. Learned, kind, wise, spiritual, and soft-spoken, he captivated the members of the temple and was immediately offered the position. Everyone was sure that even angels came to listen to the wisdom emanating from his lips.

Fortunately for the villagers, the elders of the temple were able to see past the fact that Jacob, their new brilliant young rabbi, was disfigured. A crooked spine had deformed him from birth, and he walked with a pronounced limp. Although it seemed as if he must always be in pain, his demeanor was unfailingly cheerful. And as the new spiritual leader of the town, he executed his duties better than anyone could have expected. The temple was overcrowded for services, and his students had renewed enthusiasm for their studies. The townspeople began to come to Jacob with their problems, and even Simon, the mayor, preferred Jacob's help to anyone else's when it came to both business and family matters. The young rabbi was a frequent guest at Simon's home, and the two spent hours discussing many issues.

After a year of study and service to his new community, Jacob thought it was time to take a wife. It was customary in those days for a rabbi to seek out a rich family to marry into. This provided the rabbi with the financial support to continue his studies and spiritual work, while the rich family gained prestige and honor. Everyone in town admired and respected Rabbi Jacob, but because of his affliction, few wanted to see him marry their daughter.

Miriam was the only child of Simon and Seporah. At 18, she was slim and graceful—a true vision of loveliness. Her green eyes sparkled when she smiled. Her long raven hair fell softly over her shoulders. She had creamy skin, teeth like pearls, and an enchanting laugh that made all the single young men of the village gaze at her adoringly, barely concealing their longing. In a word, she was beautiful.

Her parents were aware that there was something special about Miriam, something more than just beauty. They felt that, given their wealth and her good qualities, she was destined to marry well. They kept introducing her to young men whom they deemed appropriate candidates, but Miriam refused one suitor after another. Simon and Seporah were bewildered and somewhat frustrated by their daughter's strong will, but they knew better than to push her too hard.

One evening, they invited Rabbi Jacob for dinner, hoping he might have a solution to their dilemma. Miriam greeted their familiar guest at the door with a warm smile, guiding him into the dining room before going to join her mother in the kitchen. When the men were alone, Simon confided to Jacob that he was coming to the end of his patience with Miriam's stubbornness. He told the young rabbi that if all else failed, he would arrange a marriage for her, one that he would force her to honor, if necessary.

Jacob respectfully cautioned Simon about such an action. "Simon, you cannot force Miriam to marry someone she is not destined to be with."

Simon was visibly upset. "Seporah and I don't know what to do. We just want her to be happy."

Jacob responded gently, "Simon, I would like your permission to ask Miriam to marry me."

Simon was unprepared for the suggestion and was embarrassed by it. "Miriam is so beautiful, she can have her pick of any eligible young man despite her willfulness. Jacob, you are a wonderful young man, and the whole town would like to see you happily married. But I think your physical affliction would be difficult for a young woman like Miriam to handle."

"I know I am physically deformed," Jacob said, "but this is how the Creator shaped me, so there must be a good reason for it."

Simon stammered, "But it will be embarrassing for both of you when she turns you down. You are such a good friend to us that I can't bear the thought of your visits becoming awkward. Really, I don't think this is a good idea."

When Jacob reassured him that he was willing to take his chances, Simon got up from the table and called out to his wife and daughter. He told Miriam that Jacob needed a few words with her, then ushered Seporah into another room. Simon told Seporah what he had discussed with the rabbi. As a good mother, Seporah wanted to interfere—in her daughter's best interest, of course. But after a few moments of consideration, Simon and Seporah decided that their daughter could best handle this situation by herself. They both hoped, however, that her obstinacy would not ruin their relationship with the young rabbi.

In the dining room, Miriam sat across the table from the rabbi. As usual, she was very comfortable in his presence. Jacob asked her why she could not decide on a suitor when so many wonderful applicants had presented themselves. This question convinced Miriam that her parents had solicited the rabbi's help in trying to marry her off. The best way to deal with this was to tell Jacob the truth. She confided that many of her young suitors were nice enough and from good families; however, she knew that none of them was right for her.

"Why not?" asked Jacob.

"Because," she replied, "something is always missing."

When Jacob questioned her further, she responded, "There's no real connection between us." All these admirers had offered her relationships that guaranteed she would be cared for, even admired, yet she felt that she would also be suffocated. The right man, she explained, would make her spirit soar, and she would do the same for him. He would encourage her to grow beyond the traditional responsibilities of a wife and mother. For some reason, she felt destined to be more than the wife of a wealthy man, more than an ornament on someone's arm. She had never confided this to anyone before, but she felt safe sharing her longings with the rabbi.

Jacob silently gathered his thoughts. "I think what your heart desires, Miriam, is the other half of yourself, your soul mate." Miriam's eyes widened. "The other half of myself?" She paused for a moment, considering. "Yes, that is exactly what I have been waiting for."

"Our soul mates are not always available to us," Jacob continued. "Or they could be right in front of us, yet we might not recognize them for who they are."

Miriam sat still, waiting for the next words Jacob would offer. Jacob leaned forward and looked into Miriam's eyes. He saw beyond their color and shape, deep into her heart and through to her soul. Their connection at that instant was so intimate that it spanned lifetimes.

"Miriam," he said tenderly, "you cannot find your soul mate with your eyes, only with your heart. When you are joined on the deepest level, there will be a force, a pull between the two of you that will be incredibly strong. Whether he is a stranger from afar or someone very close to you, when you open your heart, you will know him."

Meanwhile, Simon and his wife were waiting patiently for what seemed hours. Finally, Miriam came in to see them. She smiled at her father, threw her arms around her mother, and said, "We need to plan a wedding."

Simon and Seporah were dumbfounded, but they could see that something very special had taken place between the two young people. The radiance and certainty on Miriam's face told them that she had made her decision and that she would not change her mind. Simon and his wife congratulated the couple and welcomed Jacob into their family.

When Miriam and her mother left the room to start making the wedding arrangements, Simon asked Jacob, "What did you say? How did you get her to agree?"

Jacob explained that as he and Miriam talked, it had become clear that they were soul mates who had spent many lifetimes together. In her last life, Miriam had been stubborn and proud to a fault, and her ego caused great pain to others. As a result, she was destined to come back into this life with a deformity. Knowing her and loving her as he did, Jacob had recognized that she would be unable to bear such a difficult burden, so he took upon himself the deformity that was meant for her.

Several months later, Simon and Seporah threw a splendid, festive wedding for their daughter and the young rabbi, which the entire town attended. Not only did Miriam and Jacob raise a loving, beautiful family, but Jacob also became one of the great rabbis of his generation while Miriam served the community as a pillar of strength and kindness.

This story asks us to stop and inquire into the true nature of love. How can we be sure we're with the right person? What is the role of soul mates in our lives?

What Are Soul Mates?

The Bible describes the moment God created Adam:

"And God created man in His image, in the image of God He created Him; male and female He created them." *(Genesis 1:27)*

Every soul has two halves: Male and female. This means that each and every one of us has a male or female counterpart in this world—the other half of our soul. This person is what we've come to call our soul mate. However, most of us in the world today marry to facilitate our correction, our *tikkun*, rather than connecting to our soul mate. We marry the person who will best help us with our soul's process, who will challenge us to transform. This is because most of us have not yet attained the high spiritual level that earns us reunification with the other half of our soul.

Happy is the person who is meritorious in his deeds and walks the Path of Truth, so they will unite one soul with the other, THE MALE WITH THE FEMALE, as they were before THEY CAME TO THIS WORLD. For if he is worthy in deeds, he is a complete man. BUT IF HE IS NOT MERITORIOUS, THAN HE SHALL NOT BE GIVEN HIS SOUL MATE. This is why it is written about him, "And his fruit is sweet to my taste." Because this man is blessed with reunion OF MALE AND FEMALE, AS IT SHOULD PROPERLY BE. And the world is blessed by him THROUGH HIS SWEET FRUIT, NAMELY GOODLY CHILDREN, because everything depends on whether a person's actions have been meritorious or not.

—The *Zohar, Lech Lecha* 22:208

Women are innately more spiritual than men. Even as children, women are more emotionally grounded. Yet because the feminine aspect of the soul cannot complete its process until the male aspect is also corrected, the female aspect must wait for the male to reach spiritual maturity. Sometimes this can take many lifetimes, many reincarnations. Indeed, the *Zohar* says that the female must sometimes wait a long time before her soul mate creates a spiritual environment that's right for her; this long wait is sometimes reflected in a great difference in ages when two soul mates finally reunite.

Rav Chaim Vital was a great scholar and kabbalist. He was essentially the only student of the Ari, since teaching Rav Vital was the Ari's purpose for coming into this world. Rav Vital was married when he asked his teacher, "When am I going to meet my soul mate?" The Ari answered, "When you overcome your anger [one of Rav Vital's biggest problems]. When you surmount the negative aspects of your life and become more elevated, your soul will reach the level of the soul of Rachel, the wife of Rabbi Akiva, and you will be allowed to marry her. Through that union, you will have a son."

Some time after this, Rav Vital's wife died. He married again, this time to a young woman whom he knew to have the soul of Rabbi Akiva's wife. And from that union came Shmuel Vital, the writer who went on to document the teachings the Ari transmitted through Rav Vital, including this very story.

Sometimes the female aspect of the soul waits for its male counterpart to reach the level that will allow the two individuals to be married, but sometimes the timing just isn't right on either side. Fortunately, it's not always necessary for a woman or a man to marry their true soul mate. Sometimes marrying a soul mate is required in order to get the job of correction done, and sometimes it's not. However, if souls are lucky enough or have worked hard enough on their spiritual goals, then they are allowed to marry their counterpart. This is the union of soul mates, and it reflects the fact that the two souls have been part of each other for all eternity.

Soul Mates and Conflict

Often our soul mates come from across the sea, both literally and figuratively. Two such people might have been separated by great distances and yet find each other in some unexpected way.

Or they might just be very different, a seemingly unlikely pair who meet by weird coincidence and find a cosmic dance going on between them. If this is the case, this is more likely to be a soul mate relationship than most.

As a matter of fact, the Ari says that if two people want to be together but the whole world turns upside down around them in opposition to their union—if outside there is chaos, but peace and love reign between the two of them—this is another sign that theirs must be a soul mate marriage. As we've discussed, Light comes from the negative, not from the positive. Shakespeare knew that: Just look at Romeo and Juliet!

The Unexpected Role of Death and Divorce

Every now and then, a soul mate union could occur, except that the woman is still committed to another man. In this case, there are two ways to allow the soul mate marriage to go forward. One is death and the other is divorce. In fact, Jewish law permits divorce for this just reason: To allow the first husband or wife to stand aside so that the soul mate marriage may take place. This is the explanation for the law requiring a signed bill of divorcement (a *get*). It doesn't mean that every man should divorce his wife. Rather, it means that every woman and every man needs to fulfill this precept at some point—not in each lifetime but at some point during their many lifetimes. It's part of the Taryag Mitzvot, the 613 spiritual principles contained in the Bible.

Why must we follow the *Taryag Mitzvot* and write a get? To save a life. If the husband doesn't write a *get* and stands in the way of a soul mate marriage, he dies. Indeed, under these circumstances, writing a get is a *mitzvah*—a good deed and a spiritual duty.

As the *Zohar* tells us:

> *Rav Yehuda inquired of Rav Elazar, "I am aware of the secret of this subject. THEREFORE I ASK where do those souls that are reincarnated, BUT HAVE NO SOUL MATES, find their spouses? He responded, "It is written: 'How shall we do for wives for them that remain?' (Shoftim 21:7), and "you shall catch every man his wife...." (Ibid. 21) Although this passage deals specifically with the sons of Benjamin, IT ACTUALLY DEALS WITH THE REINCARNATED SOULS, WHO MAY PRECEDE THEIR FRIENDS AND TAKE THEIR SOUL MATES AWAY FROM THEM THROUGH MERCY. Therefore, as we have learned, "Lest another precede him with Mercy."*

> *Rav Yehuda said that this is definitely the meaning of "It is difficult for the Holy One, blessed be He, to bring couples together," BECAUSE HE IS OBLIGED TO TAKE FROM ONE AND GIVE TO THE OTHER.*

> —The *Zohar, Lech Lecha* 33: 354-355

We see this situation at work in the famous biblical story of King David and Batsheva.

King David is up on a balcony of his palace when he sees a beautiful young woman bathing on the roof of a nearby house. He wants her, so he calls for her, sleeps with her, and she becomes pregnant. Then King David summons her husband, Uriah, a soldier in his army, home from battle. The king gets Uriah drunk and sends him home to bed his wife in an attempt to make it look as if Uriah has fathered the child. When Uriah refuses Batsheva, King David sends him off to the front lines where he is killed, thus freeing Batsheva to marry the king.

Okay. That's the story. If I were to read this for the first time, I would say, "What kind of a creep is this King David?" But once again everything changes when we see it through the prism of reincarnation, as the *Zohar* does.

> *King David, after what happened to him with Batsheva, was very fearful. Because at that time, Dumah (the Angel of Death) ascended to the Holy One, blessed be He, stood before Him, and said, Master of the Universe, in the Bible it says of "the man that commits adultery with another man's wife [that]...the adulterer and the adulteress shall surely be put to death." (Vayikra 20:10) Furthermore, it is written, "Moreover, you shall not lie carnally with your neighbor's wife to defile yourself with her." (Ibid. 18:20) So what is to become of David, who has profaned the Holy Covenant by committing adultery? The Holy One, blessed be He, said to him, "David is righteous! And the Holy Covenant remains*

intact, because it is known to Me that Batsheva was assigned to him since the day the world was created.

DUMAH (the Angel of Death) said to Him (Lord), If this is known to you, it is not known to him (David). He, THE HOLY ONE, BLESSED BE HE, SAID TO HIM, 'Not only that, but all that happened was permitted and done lawfully. Because every person that went to war did not leave until he had given a bill of divorce to his wife!' He said to Him, If this is so, he should then have waited for three months, which he did not! He replied: When is this applied? Only in cases where we suspect that she might be pregnant! And it is known to me for certain that Uriah never touched her.

—The *Zohar*, *Prologue* 14:132-133

King David is on the spiritual plane called *Chochmah*, one of the highest levels of spirituality and one that grants him even greater vision than a prophet. As he is standing on the balcony of his palace, he has a vision that the Temple will be built. He sees the Light of God coming into that Temple. He then looks down, sees a woman bathing next door—Batsheva—and realizes that only through her will this Temple be built. She is his soul mate, and he needs her to complete his correction. So he brings Batsheva to him.

Let's pause here for a moment to talk about names because they are significant to our understanding of this story from a kabbalistic perspective. Batsheva's name is composed of *bat*, which means "daughter," and *sheva*, which means "of seven."

The world of *Malchut*—the physical dimension that we live in—is the seventh level. Batsheva's name means "the daughter of the world of *Malchut*." She is David's soul mate because she is daugther of the Earth, a symbol of the planet, of the place of *Malchut*; and David, as we know, is the chariot of *Malchut*.

Uriah's name is also important. It means "house." He was a vessel for Batsheva, providing her with a place where she would be protected and nurtured until David reached the level of spirituality that would allow him and Batsheva to be together. Uriah took Batsheva as his own but never slept with her.

It is also said that in those days when a man went off to battle, he drew up a contingent bill of divorcement, not knowing if he would ever return home or in the event that he died in battle but his body was never found. A contingent bill of divorcement meant that as long as the husband was away at war, his wife was not his wife. This was obviously very important in the case of David and Batsheva, for it meant that they did not commit adultery.

Spiritually, great negativity befalls a woman who does commit adultery because she is a vessel. If you filled a cup with coffee, orange juice, milk, and tea, that wouldn't make a very fulfilling beverage, would it? A vessel is meant to carry only one seed, one man's DNA. If a woman carries the seed of more than the man to whom she is married, it creates negativity both for her as well as for her whole family. This is because a woman is the vessel for the family, not just for herself.

Finally, according to the kabbalistic reading of this story, Uriah went to battle and died there because the union between David and Batsheva was necessary in order for the Temple to be built.

Let's think about how this might apply to our own life. We all know people who, having lost their first spouse through death or divorce, then found and married someone wonderful. In some cases, the second marriage was far better than the first. Perhaps one reason for the dissolution of the first marriage was that the second marriage—a soul mate union—had to happen. I recently saw this principle at work in a television movie. *Loving Leah: A Levirate Marriage* is the story of a cardiologist who is persuaded to honor an ancient Jewish custom by marrying his late brother's childless widow. What at first seems like a tremendous intrusion on these two lives becomes a love story of soul mates.

As for David and Batsheva, their first child died at birth. And even though it is said that David never sinned, he washed his face with ashes every day he lived ever after, thinking that he must have done something wrong to bring this woe on himself and his wife. Batsheva's second child was Solomon, the wise king who built the Temple his father had envisioned. So David's vision did come to pass, and Batsheva was a piece of the puzzle that brought about the building of the Temple.

Different Kinds of Soul Mates

When we think of soul mates, we think of men and women being two halves of the same soul: David and Batsheva, Tristan and Isolde, Romeo and Juliet. But in the Bible, we also find the story of Jonathan and David.

The eldest son of King Saul, Jonathan was next in line for his father's throne, according to the law of the land. But Jonathan knew that David was actually supposed to be king. In fact, he loved David so much that when Saul wanted to kill David, it was Jonathan who saved David's life by alerting him to his father's plan. Jonathan was an archer. He told David he would signal his father's intentions by shooting arrows. If he shot the arrows close by, it meant that Saul had rescinded his anger. But if the arrows were shot further away, it meant that Saul's anger had not abated. When Jonathan found that the king was determined to kill David, he shot the warning arrows as they had planned.

> *After the boy had gone, David got up from the south side of the stone and bowed down before Jonathan three times, with his face to the ground. Then they kissed each other and wept together—but David wept the most. Jonathan said to David, "Go in peace, for we have sworn friendship with each other in the name of the Lord, saying, 'The Lord is witness between you and me, and between your descendants and my descendants forever.' " Then David left, and Jonathan went back to the town.*

> —*1 Samuel* 20:41-42

Despite the fact that Jonathan and David were both male, they were soul mates. In this case, there was no sexual desire for each other. They loved each other in the highest kind of friendship, but they were soul mates in the sense that they were both parts of a soul that was divided. Indeed, a soul can be divided into many aspects, not only male and female. Sexual desire does not have to be involved. Friends can also be soul mates. So can a parent and child. A soul mate relationship exists when we feel in complete harmony with another person. It can even occur between business partners. Identifying our soul mate is another piece that may fit into our puzzle.

Male and Female Souls Reversed

The *Zohar* says that when a woman is aggressive and her mate is submissive—especially during the act of sex—a female soul can sometimes choose to enter a male body that comes from this union. As recently as several decades ago, a lot of people didn't know what to think about homosexuality and gender identity issues. Today, more than ever before, it is out in the open and many of us accept it, while others continue to be challenged by it.

Reincarnation can provide the missing pieces of the puzzle that help us understand the people around us. It helps explain things that we might have found difficult to accept in the past. This is why Kabbalah explains that "knowledge is the connection." The Bible states that Adam knew Eve who bore Cain. The *Zohar* asks the question: "Why does the Bible sound so coy here? Is the

Bible too polite to mention sex?" Clearly not. There are many instances in the Bible where sex is discussed. The *Zohar* tells us that this statement about Adam and Eve that uses the term "to know" is a code, informing us indirectly that only through knowledge can we truly make a connection. This book that you're reading is a good example. Knowledge of the workings of reincarnation helps us connect to others with greater compassion, tolerance, and understanding. And it provides us with pieces of our own puzzle, bringing meaning and a sense of purpose to our lives.

Chapter 8

Helping others on their soul journey

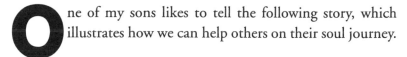

ne of my sons likes to tell the following story, which illustrates how we can help others on their soul journey.

A student once came to Rabbi Levi Itzchak of Berdichov and posed the following question: "At Passover, when we drink wine, the Haggadah says that the fifth cup is for the prophet Elijah and that those of us with merit will actually get to see him. Please, Master, I will do whatever I can. Can you tell me how I can see Elijah the Prophet this year?"

Rabbi Levi Itzchak replied, "Go and pay a visit to this small town. Spend Passover in this particular house and you will see Elijah the Prophet there."

The student was excited. He followed his teacher's directions and came to a dilapidated hovel. "Oh my," he said to himself, "I have to spend Passover here?" Still, he trusted his teacher's words and didn't want to turn back, so he knocked on the door.

The family living in this poor home invited the stranger in for Passover. The student was immediately struck by how cold it was in the house. No fire was burning. No food was cooking. So he said to the father, "You know what? I have a few rubles. Please take some to pay for firewood so you can warm your home. And here is a little more to pay for the *Seder* dinner." Noticing that the children were dressed in rags, he added, "You know what? While you're out buying food, why don't you also get some warm clothes for your children to wear? They should look good for Passover."

The student spent Passover with this family. Toward the end of the Seder, they brought out the cup for Elijah the Prophet, but no Elijah appeared. Disappointed, the young man actually slept at the table all night just in case. Nothing.

He woke up in the morning feeling depressed. At the end of the holiday, as he packed his bags, he noticed a hole in the roof so he gave the father money to fix the roof as well. Then he said his farewells and returned to Berdichov. "Master," he said when he arrived, "you promised me that I would see Elijah the Prophet, but he never came!"

"Oh, I am sorry," Rabbi Itzchak replied. "Why don't you go back to the same home for the last day of Passover, for the parting of the Red Sea. I promise you, you will see Elijah the Prophet." The student didn't have quite as much certainty in his teacher this time, but he went anyway. He returned to the small town. As he stood at the door of the hovel, about to knock, he overheard a conversation between the father and his eldest son.

"Father," the boy said, "tonight is the seventh day of Passover and we don't even have food for the table. We have nothing to serve the family. I feel really bad for Mother and all the children."

And his father replied, "Before Passover, we were in the same situation. We had nothing. But then Elijah the Prophet came and gave us money to buy food, to heat our home, to fix the roof, and to provide warm clothes for the little ones. Maybe he will come back and help us again."

Suddenly the student understood. "It's not that Elijah the Prophet is out there somewhere. Elijah the Prophet is in here...in me."

Indeed, Elijah can be found inside each and every one of us, just waiting to manifest in someone's life with a little help from us. We don't want to refuse him because of our own selfishness.

The Righteous Souls Among Us

Some righteous people reincarnate for the sake of the world. In every generation, there may be a Moses. Every generation may bring about the Final Redemption, even though we haven't achieved it yet. Still, they say that in every lifetime there are 36 righteous souls (*Lamed-Vavniks*) who hold up the world. These are good, kind souls—spiritually elevated beings who can actually leave their bodies and travel to places where there is suffering to bring healing energy. In appearance, they're just like you and me—carpenters, shopkeepers, teachers, and the like— so none of us knows who these individuals are.

Nevertheless, we are occasionally lucky enough to find that special soul, especially if there is a correction that we still haven't accomplished. Someone comes along—it could be cousin Sally from Cincinnati or just someone sitting next to us on the train—with a message that can alter our life: "Hey, guy! Straighten up and fly right." If we're open enough and attuned to hearing it, we might be at the receiving end of a helping hand from a righteous soul.

One young woman I know experienced a stillbirth: Her first baby died in *utero* at eight months. Although inconsolable, Samantha became pregnant again almost as soon as her doctors thought it was safe. When her second child was born, she felt caught in a terrible emotional bind, torn between continuing to grieve for her lost baby and her need to love this new, healthy infant.

One day, while Samantha was out with her baby on a busy city street, an old woman emerged from the throng of passersby. Peering into the stroller, this total stranger said in a thick European accent, "That baby is a gift from God." Without another word, the woman disappeared back into the crowd, leaving Samantha completely stunned. There was no way the woman could have known what this young mother had suffered, yet her words helped soothe Samantha's pain and allowed her to focus more fully on loving the baby who had survived.

A good friend of mine was having a particularly low moment. Shortly after both her mother and her dog passed away, she realized that her romantic relationship was dying, too. One morning as she was walking to the local deli to get her usual iced coffee, she suddenly felt overwhelmed by the loss of her mother and her pet. Fighting back the tears, she asked herself something, not out of acting the victim but from a genuine need to understand: "Why did this have to happen to them? Where are they now?"

Thoughts and emotions were still swirling inside her when she arrived at the deli. As she waited in line at the counter, she saw a shabbily dressed, elderly black woman. My friend somehow sensed that this woman was going to say something meaningful, that she might be a messenger for her. Suddenly the elderly lady turned toward her, looked her in the eye, and paraphrased Shakespeare.

"All the world's a stage and we are all just players. There are entrances" (she curtsied) "and there are exits." Making a grand gesture with her hands as if she were flying away, the woman then grabbed her bag from the counter and walked out, leaving my friend astonished, but oddly comforted—a feeling that only grew over time.

It can also happen that we ourselves are chosen to help someone by acting as a channel on their behalf. I am often blessed with this opportunity because of my role in The Kabbalah Centre. Many years ago, I was talking on the phone with one of our students in another city. He was telling me how things in his life had recently gone from bad to worse. At that moment, I realized that there was something I could do. I turned to one of our teachers and said, "Put some things together and get on an airplane. I want you to spend some time with John."

"All right, I'm on it," the teacher replied. He flew to John's side and spent time with him, time that truly changed John's life. I was only a catalyst in this case, but if I hadn't heard his pain, I don't know what would have happened to John. Fortunately, I had the good fortune to be there at the right moment. It is written that you can save your world—or lose it—in a minute. This was one of those instances where I was able to help save someone else, which made me feel really good.

Recently, I heard a lovely story about a taxi driver who was dispatched to pick up an elderly woman. He got to the house and waited and waited, but she didn't emerge from her home. Finally after ten minutes, he decided to go to her door. He knocked and a frail old lady came out and asked for help carrying a suitcase. Then she told the taxi driver she would like to visit her old neighborhood. So she directed him here and there, and together they went to visit all the places where important moments in her life had taken place—where she was born, where she grew up, where she shared a first kiss. After several hours, the woman handed the cabbie a paper with an address: Her final destination. As he pulled up to the curb, the cabbie realized it was a hospice. He turned off the meter, helped the lady and her bag into the building, and refused to accept payment for the considerable fare.

Imagine if he hadn't knocked on her door but had simply left. He would have missed what he called "the best day of my life." The truth is we just don't know what opportunities will come our way or even what they will look like. Sometimes it will be our role to receive a message and sometimes we will serve as messengers for someone else. This is why we need to leave ourselves open.

What's in a Name?

The word *neshama*, which means "soul," has as its root the word *shem* (name). This clue helps us to understand that our soul's job is inextricably linked to our name. Thus, when we name a newborn, we should use this opportunity to connect the child to a righteous person who lived a long life and became a spiritually enlightened being. The name will support the child with the positive energy that this righteous soul revealed and will help the child along his or her journey.

The flip side of this is also true. If we name a child after someone who has suffered, we attach an aspect of suffering to the work of that child's soul. Yet people do this all the time. For instance, they'll say, "I want to name my daughter after my mother because she died of cancer when I was very young." Yes, I understand that they want to preserve the memory of their mother, but at the same time, they risk passing some of her karma onto the child. That's why I wouldn't want to name a child after my Aunt Millie, who succumbed to injuries from a car accident at the age of 38. By doing so, I might unwittingly be opening up a space for misfortune to befall that child in the form of an accident.

When my friend Chuck told me that he was wounded in the first Gulf War, I asked him about his injuries and noted how well he had healed. Then I inquired, "Oh, by the way, how did you get your name?" He answered, "My father named me after his buddy, Charlie, who died in the Vietnam War. In fact, when I got hurt, I was the same age as Charlie when he was killed."

An interesting coincidence? Or something more?

Changing Our Name = Changing Our Karma

If it so happens that you've been named after someone whose life was filled with negative energy, this can be corrected by redirecting that energy. For instance, if you were named Miriam after your grandmother who had a serious genetic disease, you could retain your name but bring to it the energy of the prophetess Miriam, Moses' sister. By consciously focusing on the prophetess's energy, that consciousness, rather than on your grandmother's, you can redirect things in a positive way. If your name doesn't correspond to the name of an enlightened soul, another option you have is to take on a soul name—a name that supports your soul's work. You can do this through your rabbi or priest, your spiritual teacher, or any person whose consciousness you trust and who is involved in your spiritual growth.

Modern Medical Miracles

At the time the *Zohar* was written, there was little sophisticated medical knowledge. Today, with blood transfusions, organ transplants, and the like, many questions arise about the impact on one's karma of receiving body parts from others—dead or alive—and of making organ donations. Some of these questions are not easily answered because these procedures were unknown during the Ari's lifetime and therefore never written about. But I'd like to address this issue here because the donation of an organ or blood—while a tremendous act of generosity—may also alter the karma of the recipient. This is particularly true when seen in the light of reincarnation. For instance, it is written that when the Messiah comes, we will first be resurrected with all of our frailties and then we will be cured. But what happens if we no longer have a liver or a heart because it was donated to save someone else's life?

And what about an autopsy? This procedure certainly damages, and sometimes destroys, the body. Think of it this way: Pathologists cut open the body as if they were gutting a deer, and then remove all the internal organs. They measure and test them, then replace them in the body, although not necessarily where they belong. That's the reason kabbalists are opposed to autopsies.

In some instances, I feel it may be acceptable to donate or receive an organ, while in others, I'm not so sure, even if it means saving a life. Let's look at these issues a bit more closely.

Kidney and Liver Transplants

If I had a daughter who needed a kidney and mine was a match, would I give her one? Of course, I would because I have two kidneys. Am I affecting her karma? Yes, I am, but in this situation, I would do it because I'd be saving her life without sacrificing the integrity of my own body. The same is true with the liver. If doctors take a piece of human liver and donate it to a matched recipient, the donor's liver will regenerate. In both these examples, we can give someone an organ or part of one and still stay alive. Our bodies will be viable at death. The same holds true for a blood transfusion; after we donate blood, our bodies replace it.

Heart Transplants

For me, organ donation enters a grey area when we take vital organs from someone who has already finished their journey and allow those organs to continue on in someone else's cosmic sphere. All that we are karmically, all we've ever thought and been through in our lives, leaves its imprint on the organs of our body, making the question of a heart transplant a complicated one. Medically, the heart is just a pump, a muscle, however remarkable. Yet some people feel that the seeds of emotion also lie in the heart, which means it's possible that if I literally give my heart to someone else, I will also be giving that person a large part of my karma. So although I would be helping someone medically by donating my heart, I might be infringing on their purpose for coming here in the first place.

So we ask the question: "What are we supposed to do? Let the person die?" The answer to that is no, but the dilemma remains. Imposing our karma on someone else breaks a cosmic law.

Moreover, it's one thing for you to designate while you're alive that your organs can be harvested for others at your death. It's another thing entirely for family members to donate a loved one's organs after the person passed away because in this case, the family is now making a decision that the deceased person may not have desired or agreed to.

Chapter 9

Understanding death and resurrection

Sometimes we have friends over to our house for a meal together or to just sit and enjoy an afternoon or evening simply making small talk perhaps, but small talk that's pleasurable. These are good people, and we have fun together. Then they leave, and suddenly our house feels a little empty. What is this emptiness? The furniture, carpeting, artwork, and appliances are still in place, but once our friends have gone home, it feels as if something important is missing.

This is what happens—only much more intensely—when somebody leaves this world. Suddenly their energy is gone. We miss the person and feel that loss even more keenly because his or her death seems so final. We think we are never going to see our loved one again. But when we truly understand what happens in the process of death and reincarnation, then we're not quite so saddened by the passing of a friend or family member. Nor are we quite so afraid of dying ourselves.

In an earlier chapter of this book, we found that only by going through difficult challenges do we become who we need to be. Although death is obviously a huge challenge, when a person passes away, there is no end to his or her opportunities to move to a higher level. Indeed, the reason most of us fear death is because we haven't yet finished our job in this lifetime.

Grief

Grief is a long process that most people go through because they believe that death is final. Actually, people aren't usually grieving for the dead as much as they are for themselves and for the others—the living—left behind. They grieve for the emptiness that death brings to their lives: "I'm grieving because I lost my best friend. I don't have her to talk to anymore. I can't call her to tell her about my day. I feel so alone without her. I miss her so much."

Grief is personal, and therefore it's relative. We don't grieve the same way over a young mother cut down in the prime of life as we do for an elderly loved one who has been lingering in pain for many years or has been rendered unresponsive by a stroke or Alzheimer's disease. When this person passes, there is sadness, yes, but often we consider that for him or her, it's better that the struggling and suffering are over. We will still feel that sense of loss, but we can also experience a feeling of relief.

Is there a good way to grieve? Look at what his friends did for Rav Shimon, the author of the *Zohar*, the day he died.

> *Rav Shimon rose and sat down, laughed and rejoiced. He said, "Where are the friends?" Rav Elazar rose and let them in, and they sat before him. Rav Shimon raised his hands, recited a prayer and was glad. They said, "Let the friends that were present at the assembly, NAMELY THE IDRA RABA, come here." They all left, and Rav Elazar, his son, Rav Aba, Rav Yehuda, Rav Yossi, and Rav Chiya stayed. In the meanwhile Rav Yitzchak entered. Rav Shimon said to him, "How deserved is your portion. How much joy should be added to you on this day." Rav Aba sat behind him and Rav Elazar before him.*

Rav Shimon said, "Now it is time of goodwill, and I want to come without shame into the World to Come. Here are holy matters that I have not revealed until now. I wish to reveal them before the Shechinah so it shall not be said that I have gone from this world in want—until now they have been hidden in my heart, so I can enter through them into the World to Come."

—The *Zohar, Ha'azinu* 6:25-26

Yes, Rav Shimon's friends made a big party—a joyful celebration of the continuity of life.

Wakes, Cremation, and Burials

When someone dies, the Irish throw a wake. They dress up the deceased and place him or her in the middle of the room. Friends and family come to say goodbye, putting mementos in the casket and saying prayers. There is revelry and merry-making, celebration, and even dancing. The idea is to "wake up" the soul from its slumber, to keep it from losing consciousness. This way, the soul goes on living in the new dimension it's now entering. A wake usually lasts three days. Christ died and rose on the third day, so Catholics wait three days for burial.

Kabbalists, on the other hand, bury their dead immediately. The reason for this can be found in the spiritual concept of empty space. Kabbalistically, empty space is not a positive thing. It creates room for negativity to enter. Therefore a body devoid of a soul is an invitation to negative entities or angels to invade. This is why we not only bury the deceased as quickly as possible but also why, from the moment a person's soul leaves until the individual is buried, he or she is never left alone.

Some people cremate bodies. To kabbalists, however, this means that the soul's work in this lifetime cannot count as finished. The soul needs to come back to face the same corrections again, no question about it. Another reason kabbalists also don't cremate the dead is because we see cremation as a denial of the fact that this body was a vessel that held Light in it and, as such, something that needs to be respected. Also, if a body is cremated or needs to go through an autopsy, this means that this is not the final incarnation for this body. Another incarnation will take place. Moreover, we know that when our soul leaves at death, it leaves behind a spark of itself in the body at the gravesite. When we visit a righteous person at their grave, we are connecting not to their completed soul but to the spark that still resides in the remains of that physical body.

Luz Bone and Resurrection

We all have a little bone at the top of our spinal column, which in Hebrew is called the *Luz* bone. This is the spiritual instrument within our body that connects us with the Light and allows us to start over again—our pilot Light, if you will. If, God forbid, a catastrophe occurred, the world was destroyed, and humankind needed to start over again, or if the

Resurrection of the Dead came to pass, this would happen through the energy of that *Luz* bone.

So what about the person who is cremated? Now there is no body—and therefore no Luz bone. If, between the time of cremation and the soul's next incarnation (in effect, while the soul is looking for a space or vessel to occupy), the Resurrection takes place and the Messiah comes, then the Light would have nothing in the cremated body to use as a conduit. The spark would remain in the Lower World, unable to elevate because it has no vessel in which to do so.

Christianity describes the space between death and judgment, between Heaven and Hell, as purgatory. There are lots of souls in this transitional space, which is why Christianity refers to many kinds of spirits, negative and positive, that are forced to wander. From a kabbalistic perspective, these spirits wander for lack of a suitable vessel into which to reincarnate. If their previous vessel was cremated, it can no longer provide the appropriate soul with a new home. The soul can become a new body eventually, but the cremation prolongs the process. And cremation can have an effect on the way in which the soul reincarnates.

Connecting with the Dead

Many people want to connect with their loved ones who have passed away. I certainly understand this urge, but I don't recommend trying to connect with the dead, even though it may be possible to do. Why? Because our energy can interfere

...to be continued...

with what these souls are doing in their current incarnations. And more importantly, we were put here to live our own lives. We need to let our loved ones move on and move on ourselves.

Part III

Putting It All Together

Chapter 10

Assembling your puzzle pieces

Before the very beginning of everything, in what Kabbalah calls the Endless World, two forces contributed to Creation. One was the Light, the infinite, constant Desire to Share. The Light is all good. It is the universal energy that exists within everything—energy that has intelligence. *It is the Lightforce of the Creator from which our souls differentiated themselves when we were born, and it is the Lightforce to which our souls return when our bodies die. It is the Light of God.*

The ancient kabbalists define the Lightforce, called God, as infinitely giving, infinitely imparting, infinitely fulfilling. It's the energy of peace and clarity; of health and financial abundance; of affirmation, love, and relationships; of every blessing we could ever hope for. In fact, when we use the word "Light," we mean everything we can possibly imagine that is wonderful.

The purpose of studying Kabbalah is to learn how we can connect to the Light and receive all its infinite blessings. Kabbalah helps us understand that we can glean Light from everything. In fact, the moment we accept that our soul is part of the flow of Light and we tune in to that flow, everything around us will be illuminated.

The Light is pure sharing, but in the Endless World, the Light needed something on which to bestow its beneficence. So it created an entity whose capacity was so vast that it could continuously and endlessly receive all that the Light had to give; it created an infinite receiver. In Kabbalah, we call this the original soul, or the original Vessel. If the Light is plus energy, then the Vessel is minus energy, and it is the second force of Creation.

Why did the kabbalists use the word "Vessel"? The Vessel was the original being created for the sake of receiving all the pleasures and goodness that the Creator and the Light wanted to give. In the same way that a cup holds water, each of us is a vessel, a container with the capacity to receive what the Creator has in store for us.

The Vessel was the result of the Light's desire to share. And the Vessel wanted everything the Light had to offer, every form of desire. So for a while, there was complete harmony. The sharing nature was sharing: The Light gave. The receiving nature was receiving: The Vessel got. And it was perfect!

But things changed.

In any creation, you find the essence of its creator. Although the nature of the Vessel was solely to receive, upon being imbued with the outpouring of love from the Creator, the Vessel also absorbed the Light's sharing nature. In the Endless World, the Vessel was being given everything—everything, that is, except the chance to give in return, and thereby actually earn the Light it was receiving. But receiving without reciprocating began to make the Vessel more and more uneasy as it, in itself, developed the desire to give and share. But the Light is only about giving; It didn't have the capacity to receive. So the Light said to the Vessel, "I cannot take anything from you."

By now, the Vessel could not continue to receive without sharing. Our universe came about as a result of the Vessel saying, "I feel ashamed. I'm getting something for nothing" (in kabbalistic terms, this is called Bread of Shame), "and I must have the opportunity to share as well."

So the Vessel pushed back and resisted the Light. It said to the Light, "STOP! NO MORE!" Since the Creator's only intention was to please the Vessel, the Creator withdrew the Light. In Kabbalah, we say that the Light *restricted* itself, creating a moment of such utter darkness that it was unbearable for the Vessel. Sensing this, the Light rushed back in at full force, but the Vessel wasn't ready for it. At that instant, the Vessel shattered exploding into an infinite number of fragments, thereby creating all of the souls of humanity, as well as time, space, motion, and the physical universe as we know it today. The Big Bang!

The *Zohar* teaches us: As Above, so Below. What existed in the Endless World also exists on Earth. All the fragments of our universe, including our souls, contain some aspect of the Desire to Receive. In fact, this desire to receive is essential. It's the engine that drives everything in the universe.

However, there's an all-important difference between the Desire to Receive and the Desire to Receive for the Self Alone. Every time we receive energy selfishly, allowing our desire to receive to control us, without restricting ourselves or giving something in return, we partake of Bread of Shame. We still receive the energy we demand, which fills us up for a moment and creates the rush we crave in the short run. But then it short-circuits, and instead of joy, we find negativity and chaos in our lives.

The Desire to Receive for the Self Alone separates our soul from the source of the Light. Think about your life. When you indulge in instant gratification, when you fail to make an effort, when you're not initiating or taking responsibility, when you just go with whatever's easiest, when you're lazy or you procrastinate—we kabbalists would say that, at that moment, you're disconnected from the Light. You're acting from a Desire to Receive for the Self Alone when it's all about "me, me, me!"

The purpose of reincarnation is to give us the opportunity to become proactive with our sharing. It's about consciousness. In fact, our consciousness helps determine how much Light our Vessel can handle. If our consciousness is all about "me, me, me," then our ability to receive the Light—our vessel—will be quite small. Only big enough for one, in fact. But if we think about looking after the whole planet, imagine how big our vessel would be then, and how much Light we could contain! That kind of consciousness heals people and allows them to experience a truly fulfilling life.

So ask yourself, "How can I change my situation to be in the Light?" The only way is by acting like the Light. That means giving and creating. And being a creator means being the cause, being the initiator, being *proactive*. Our physical world was created to give us the opportunity, we did not have in the Endless World, to become beings who share, not just passive receivers.

Indeed, our soul's real purpose in each lifetime is to transform that part of our nature that is the Desire to Receive for the Self Alone into the Desire to Receive for the Sake of Sharing. That's when our soul returns to its source—the Light. In kabbalistic terms, this requires us to restrict: To be there for other human beings when they need us. To leave our comfort zone to help them. This is when the Light of the Creator can flow through us and create miracles.

Learning to transform our Desire to Receive for the Self Alone into the Desire to Receive for the Sake of Sharing is the purpose of each of our incarnations.

We have many lifetimes to reconnect with the original circuitry of love. This is why it's so important to understand reincarnation. Kabbalah helps us see the grand puzzle—the Light and the Vessel. But it also helps us understand our individual puzzles—the purpose of our own lives. Each of us comes into this world with a different aspect to correct. This book is meant to help you put together the pieces to facilitate your own correction.

From Kabbalah, we understand that we have been here before and that our souls have returned to this world to help us improve upon the shortcomings of our earlier lives. Kabbalah helps us to understand our puzzle—who we are in this lifetime and our *tikkun*—by providing us with three powerful tools: Angels, kabbalistic astrology, and face and palm reading. In the rest of Part III, you will learn about these tools and how to apply them to your life. Refer to these tools often, as they can help you along in your journey back to the Light.

Tools

Angels

I had a wild childhood. I went to 13 public schools in 12 years. I didn't learn how to read until I was in the eighth grade. I wore so many different clothes I didn't always recognize that they were mine. I ran through so many lifetimes in those short years that at one point, I didn't even know which body I fit into. The other kids, of course, made fun of me. In the fifth or sixth grade, they got really upset with me. They tied me up and threw me into a pit where I stayed the night. I was terrified. I was a kid. I didn't know what the heck to do.

But in that frightening darkness, I heard a voice say to me, "Don't worry. You're going to be doing great things in your life."

Well, who the heck are you? I thought. *What's going on here?*

Then I saw a figure. I felt him, too. It was an angel. He said, "My name is Michael. Don't worry. The reason you have the life you have is so that you'll be able to understand people. You will be put through many tests to see whether you can be the one to help others."

We went on to have a whole conversation. "Nobody understands me," I said. "Everybody thinks I'm weird. They think I'm crazy."

"Just don't worry," Michael repeated. "It won't last forever."

"So why do I have to stay here in this pit?" I asked.

Again he said, "Don't worry. They'll find you in the morning and you'll be fine. Nothing is going to happen to you tonight. And anytime you need me, just close your eyes and ask. I'll come to you."

It was the most amazing experience and one of the most profound in my life. I don't think an adult could have had an encounter like this, but children are more open, more connected to the Light. I've been through similar incidents since that time, but that was my all-important introduction to my angel, Michael. Today, I can sit by myself in a room, and it's as if he's standing there next to me. But I know that how he looks to me may not be how he looks to someone else he may visit.

Once, when I had my astrology chart done, the astrologer said to me, "I don't know what it is that I'm seeing. It looks like you could run through fire and not get burned." And I know that's true because I *have* run through fire. But I'm here to tell this story, thanks to my friend, the archangel Michael.

What Are Angels?

In every culture, we hear stories about ethereal beings. Some people call them angels. They are with us, within us, and around us. In fact, every human being has spiritual guides that can take many forms. So the question becomes: What are angels anyway?

We could think of them as spiritual energies. Kabbalah teaches that the infrastructure of our universe is composed of billions of angels. Angels can enter into our bodies; indeed, they are part of our bodies. Although angels have the ability to take human shape, they may also appear with six massive wings. Or they can show up as minute bits of energy known as molecules. Everything in this world is energy, and angels are no exception.

What Do Angels Do?

You may have heard about the archangel Raphael, who is the angel of healing; Michael, the angel of mercy; Gabriel, the angel of justice; and Uriel, who can bring balance into our lives. These archangels can each lead us in a certain direction, but it's up to us whether we follow their guidance.

Each angel has its own specific singular job. You won't hear about angels multitasking. For instance, one angel does nothing but bring the sea to the shore; that's its job. Other angels inspire flowers to bloom. The angel, Dumah, takes our souls away from this world when we die. Unlike people, angels won't interfere with each other's tasks. To each their own. And unlike humans, angels don't have free will. They just do as they're instructed by more powerful angels or by the Creator.

We ourselves create angels with our actions during the week, which makes angels very much a part of our everyday lives. Just as we have different support systems in the physical world (friends, family, doctors, etc.), so, too, do we have systems for help in the spiritual world. For example, the angels that assist us every day act as a kind of governor of that day. (I have included a list of those angels at the end of this section.) Their names are formed in the ancient language of Aramaic, but we don't speak them out loud. We simply scan the Aramaic letters with our eyes and ask a given angel for help on that day. (Just as with our cell phones, we may not completely understand this technology, but we can still use it to improve our lives, which is more important than knowing exactly how the tool works.) There are also ways we can call on our guardian angel for help, too, if we are inclined to do so. I'll explain how later in this section.

Negative Angels

Everything in life is based on polarity. You have positive (white) angels and negative (dark) angels. But in the spiritual world, like attracts like. So when we live our lives properly, when we don't get involved with the negative side, we attract white angels. But if we live our lives negatively, we attract dark angels. And we can be sure that the negative side is always lurking around, waiting to rush to our side when we make a mistake.

As for those dark angels, it's best not to pronounce their names. This only makes them more effective at their job: manifesting chaos. The female dark entity is often the source of negativity that comes to children; croup and sudden infant death syndrome are just two examples of her handiwork.

Earlier in this book, I mentioned the dangers of drinking directly from a stream without using a cup or other vessel.

There are also other ways of innocently absorbing the energy of dark forces. I once walked under the shade of a big tree on a Friday night, and a very disturbing feeling came over me so I ran right back into the house. Later I learned that certain negative angels hide in the darkness of shade trees. They lie in wait for people to walk by so they can corrupt them. Did you ever think, *"I don't know what got into me. I would never say that!"* Well, sometimes it's because you've been influenced. This is the spiritual reason why it's a bad idea to walk alone at night. You're not only vulnerable to physical dangers but to spiritual ones as well.

Were negative angels created by God? The answer is no. When Adam and Eve were created, they were put into the Garden of Eden. Had Adam not eaten from the Tree of Knowledge of Good and Evil, we would have remained in the world of eternity. But Adam and Eve chose the world of the finite, and when they fell into this world, they were joined by the negative side, which brought with it a legion of negative angels. These dark angels are created by our own negativity, our destructive actions. The same is true of positive angels, except that they're the product of our positive actions.

There is a saying: "If you allow me to lead you, I will help you to the Light. But if you decide not to go to the Light, you'll also get all the help you need to go the other way." This implies that an angel is like a being with a spotlight that allows you to drive. It's there to tell you, "I don't think you ought to go this way." But it's up to you to hear that advice—and to decide whether or not to take it.

Mercy and Judgment

Mercy and Judgment—*Chesed* and *Gevurah*—are also twin poles of the universe. Through our actions, we vacillate between them. We earn mercy and advance our process of correction through acts of sharing and loving kindness, but we bring judgment upon ourselves when we allow our ego to run the show.

> *As we have learned, everything in the world has a voice, and an angel which floats and flies in the firmament, where those winged creatures catch it and carry it aloft to be judged to good or to evil, as it is written: "For the bird of Heaven shall carry the sound and that which has wings shall tell the matter." (Ecclesiastes 10:20)*
>
> —The *Zohar, Lech lecha* 34:358.

Angels listen, and they take our thoughts, our words, and our actions to the Upper Chambers in the spirit world. If we have engaged in positive actions, thoughts, or spoken words, angels may return the favor by whispering a positive message about us in the ear of a boss, a date, or a policeman on the verge of giving us a ticket. On the other hand, if we indulge in negative thoughts, words, or actions, like-minded angels will hide our keys or obscure our vision so we miss seeing that obstacle and bang into it with our car.

Angels as Messengers

In the New Testament, the birth of Jesus was heralded by angels who said he would be called the "king of the Jews." So we know that biblically speaking, angels were messengers. I try to leave myself open as much as I can to receive messages that angels may send me. In cases when I've needed supernal support, I've placed a chair in the room for the prophet Elijah, who often appears when a message has to be delivered. When Jacob sent Joseph out of the house to visit his brothers, Joseph couldn't find them at first, but he met a man along the way who directed him; that man was Elijah the Prophet.

That's one form of angel. Here is another. Many years ago, the Rav and I heard a knock at our door. When we opened it, an old woman was standing there. She asked us for bread—not for money, just for bread. There was something very strange about her. When we compared notes later, it turned out that we were having the same awed thought: *This isn't really a human being, is it?* Still, we filled a care package with everything we had to give. We made sandwiches for her. Cheeses. Fruit. Then right after she left, we thought, *Why didn't we offer her some money, too?* I remember that the Rav ran downstairs to offer her some, but she was gone. She was a very old woman who could barely walk, but in just a few moments, she had disappeared. We couldn't find her anywhere.

I took this incident to mean that something had been about to happen to us that may not have been so pleasant. But this angel came to our door to see what we would do. By being generous with no thought of return, we must have passed the test, and the angel protected us.

These things really happen. Not just to me. Spiritual interventions occur in everyone's life. In fact, a story in the *Zohar* illustrates this very point.

Two students of Rav Shimon were walking in the wilderness when they came upon three people in the midst of a "situation." Something told the students to hide behind a tree and observe what was going on. They saw two travelers who had met a man who had lost his way in the forest and was starving.

One of the travelers said, "Well, I'm going to help him."

But the other said, "You know, we have a long walk ahead of us, and you won't make it if you give him your food. You won't have enough to eat yourself. You're going to die in the wilderness if you help this man. So it's your life or his."

But the first traveler ignored his friend's warning and gave the hungry man his food.

One of the two students of Rav Shimon wanted to reveal himself to the travelers and save the day. But the other student said, "No, no. This is an act of Heaven. We have to see what's going to happen next." So they decided to follow this pair as they made their way through the wilderness.

As the day wore on, the generous traveler weakened. But rather than showing him kindness and compassion, his friend said, "I told you this would happen." Having a selfish nature, he continued on his way, leaving his companion to die alone in the middle of nowhere. The weak traveler stumbled, leaned against a tree, and eventually fell asleep. While he slept, a snake slid down the tree trunk and prepared to bite him. But an angel in the form of another snake came down and grabbed the deadly snake by its head, saving the traveler's life.

At this point, the students of Rav Shimon stepped out from behind the cover of the trees. They awakened the generous traveler, fed him, and told him what they had observed. "You see," they explained, "you were about to die. But the angels had given you an opportunity with the starving stranger to act out of kindness—and because you had been so generous, you were allowed to live."

—The *Zohar, Behar* 9:58-62

Certain situations in our lives that might seem very difficult if viewed by someone else are oftentimes interventions from Above. They create a circumstance that can determine whether we move forward with our process or stall out. Any stranger who asks something of us could be deciding whether or not to give us a message or to intervene on our behalf. Because what is an angel? It's a messenger, after all.

Angels, Speech, and Consciousness

Consciousness has energy just like everything else in the universe, but most of the time, we lose sight of this fact. If you want to test the truth of what I've said, try this little exercise. The next time you go to the movies, stare at the back of the neck of the person sitting in front of you. Just focus on a spot on his or her neck, and sooner or later, that person is going to start touching that spot and may even turn around to face you. Why? Because that person can feel the energy from your eyes.

Words have energy, too. Sometimes when we gossip a little, it may seem as if we're saying things of little importance. But every word we utter gets amplified by an angel. Angels are channels. They are part of the wiring system that links our world and the Upper World. Once we become aware of this mechanism, we begin to speak and act differently. Now we're far more reluctant to lose our tempers and say nasty things we will later regret. Whereas before we might have said, "Get away from me!" or "I hate you!" or "I wish you were dead!" in a moment of anger, now we know that angels are waiting to pass those words on—and may even make the sentiment behind the words come to pass. Once we're aware that our words have energy, we know there may be an angel with a sword standing next to the people we really love.

Being conscious means knowing that everything we do or say has an effect, negative or positive. Just because we don't see the result right away doesn't mean it isn't coming. On the contrary. People who are very attuned to the spiritual aspects of life realize that there isn't a blade of grass that grows without an angel telling it to grow.

Can we maintain this heightened consciousness all the time? Probably not. The Ari says that if we were able to truly see everything around us—all the energies and forces at work beyond the reach of our five senses—we would probably die of fright!

The Archangels

Although the universe is filled with billions of angels, there are only four permanent archangels: Raphael, Michael (Mikhail), Gabriel, and Uriel. They are the commanders-in-chief, the master fleet builders. Our champions. Let's look at them a bit more closely.

Raphael

Raphua means "to cure" in Hebrew, and Raphael is the angel of healing. Kabbalah teaches that disease means dis-ease. When you are ill physically, something is out of balance spiritually. Nothing happens in the physical realm that doesn't occur first in the metaphysical world. Think of the spiritual world as a computer and the physical world as a printer. The real decisions are made using the computer's software. Those decisions then manifest physically on the computer screen as words or images, which can then be printed on a piece of paper. But if you need to correct the text, you must go back to the computer, fix the error, and then reprint the document.

In the spiritual world, decisions are made at the level of consciousness. Sickness, therefore, would arise from that level, too, so that is where it must be addressed. One option is to call upon the archangel Rafael.

Michael

Given the story of my childhood, it's easy to understand why my favorite angel is Michael. He's the angel of mercy, or *Chesed*. Michael is king of the archangels. His name means "Who is as God." He is the angel to call upon when you seek repentance, righteousness, and above all, mercy. We are bounced between Mercy and Judgment—Chesed and Gevurah. Mercy is the force that softens judgment, and Michael is a warrior for that goodness.

Gabriel

Gabriel is the angel of judgment. It is said of him that he holds the wheel of life and death. He decides—based on the incarnation that just ended and the life that is to be—which soul goes into which vessel at conception and when it is time for a soul to leave its body behind. The archangel Gabriel is the angel of the wheel of life; he is the soul-bearer.

Gevurah means "strength," and we can see a common root in the words *gevurah* and Gabriel. Gabriel's name means "Strength of God." Judgment is Gabriel's domain, so we must be careful of him. According to ancient scripture, the Creator instructed Gabriel to "go and write signs on the foreheads of the righteous so no sabotage angels can harm them. Go to the evil ones and write signs on their foreheads so sabotage angels can harm them."

So Gabriel, our judge, marks an invisible "R" for righteousness on our forehead when we curb our self-centered nature, resist reactive behavior, and advance our process. That mark is a celestial seal of approval. Destructive angels take one look and leave us in peace. But if we are mired in negativity, Gabriel gives us a different mark. Then, as the ancient text says, "the sabotage angels" will wreak their justice on us.

I certainly wouldn't want to get too close to Gabriel because his job is judgment. It's about life and death. It is his decision to use the wheel of life without the grace of God because it is Gabriel who has final control of it.

The beginning of the Bible chapter of Vayera states: "And God appeared...and Abraham was sitting at the entrance of the tent...and he saw three men standing nearby." (Genesis 18:1-2) The three "men" were angels, and each had one mission to accomplish. The *Zohar* explains that God sent these archangels to minister to Abraham who was 90 years old and just recovering from the circumcision he had performed on himself. But who were these three archangels?

Raphael, the healer, came to ease Abraham's physical suffering and heal his circumcision, for this was the third and most difficult day. Michael came to bless Abraham and Sarah, who would bear a child the following year. And Gabriel, bringer of judgment and justice, came to tell Abraham that the cities of Sodom and Gomorrah, which were wracked by evil, would be destroyed.

Uriel

We want balance in our lives, and this balancing act is the job of the archangel Uriel. It is written that "Uriel watches over thunder and terror." The name Uriel means "Fire of God," but the word is derived from the Hebrew word or, which means "light." So Uriel can also be called "Light of God." He is the great balancer and a powerful force to bring into our life.

Some of us are extremely emotional, others extremely intellectual or judgmental. Still others among us may be mired in numbness. Uriel brings balance and helps us to moderate our behavior, even in our numbness.

Call upon the names of these archangels: Raphael, Michael, Gabriel, Uriel. Say their names aloud. See if there's one in particular with whom you connect, from whom you feel energy.

Metatron

Metatron is unique in the hierarchy of angels because he is the only one to have begun life as a human being. Through spiritual work and transformation, he not only ascended to angelic status, but was taken away in a chariot and made head of all the angels. Originally known as Enoch, or Chanoch, when he was mortal, he was given the name Metatron after being transformed into an angel.

The *Zohar* identifies Metatron as the angel who led the people of Israel through the wilderness after their exodus from Egypt. Metatron transmits the daily orders of God to the archangel Gabriel, as well as to Satan, the angel of death. When Metatron was given the job of overseeing all the angels, they became angry and asked the Creator, "How could you put a man over us?" And the Creator replied, "Because an angel does not have a desire to receive and because you have only one task in this world, which you perform without free will; you cannot make decisions by yourself." Metatron, by contrast, had lived as a human. He had seen it all and had used his free will to be part of God. Even after all the suffering he went through, he chose to devote his life entirely to the Creator. By virtue of this enormous accomplishment, he was allowed to rise above the angels.

As the *Zohar* tells us in the biblical portion of Chaye Sarah, the angels also expressed their unhappiness with Creation. They asked God, "Why are You going to create the world? You know that man is going to sin and cause suffering. Why would You do this?" And the Creator responded, "Because that's part of what life is all about. You won't ever experience that aspect of life, but you can help Me lift up those who have fallen."

We Can Be Prompted

Sometimes in the quiet of night, if you listen carefully enough, you might be able to hear the flutter of a wing. Yes, it's true: Each one of us can learn to hear the angels.

This process of listening to the angels' voice inside us is governed by our consciousness. Oftentimes it's the voice of an angel that is guiding us by saying, "You know you don't want to do that." Sometimes we connect with more than just a voice; we can actually feel the presence of an angel, as I did with Michael that night in the pit.

Yet all too often, we block out the voice or the presence. Perhaps we're afraid, or perhaps the voice is saying something we don't want to hear. But if we allow ourselves to experience the spiritual dimension, we can become much more useful conduits for Light in the world and the universe.

There's a poem about an astronomer and a boy in which the astronomer devotes himself to measuring the stars: How far away they are, how long it takes for their light to reach us. But the boy simply drinks in the glorious light shining and blazing as if through pinpricks in the blanket of night sky. When we think about angels, we should try to be more like the boy than the astronomer.

I'm not saying we should go through life free of rational thought. But if we want this energy, this ability to understand angels, we have to open ourselves to it by temporarily letting go of our rational mind's dominance. Kabbalistically, if we leave space with the intention of allowing a positive energy force to enter, we can receive a gift in the form of an elevated visitor. The best way to do this is to encourage our rational mind to stand aside, leaving us to fill our consciousness with this other energy.

Try to sit quietly for 20 minutes a day (I know that's a lot) and push everything out of your mind. Just breathe and listen to the quiet. Then pay attention to whatever comes to mind. See if you can develop the ability first to recognize and then to speak to your inner voice, perhaps connecting more fully with the particular being that's there for you. It's a possibility. Try it and see.

Your Guardian Angel

We each have our own guardian angel, and each guardian angel has its own name. Our angel may not come to us with a name, but in that case, we can just give it one. In truth, it's not as important to know our guardian angel's name as it is to know that our angel exists—and that it is always with us.

At the moment we are born, our personal guardian angel taps us on the lip, creating the little groove between our nose and our mouth. With that blow, we forget most everything we knew before, including whatever glimpse we were given of our assembled puzzle.

...to be continued...

Our guardian angel escorts our soul into this world at birth and leaves us only when we die. It travels alongside us throughout the journey of our life, providing tests that help us complete our process and nudging us if we're veer from the path. Our angel is our teacher, friend, and foe—in short, our spiritual partner in this life. Our guardian angel helps us put the pieces of our puzzle together. The more we open ourselves to our angel's influence, the higher we can reach.

Guardian angels help us gain access to spiritual levels we can't achieve on our own merits. They make the connections. Their purpose is to bring Light into our physical world of confusion and questions. They use their influence to intercede on our behalf. They are like benevolent personal attorneys, negotiating to bring us the best deal for our spiritual growth. When we go through difficult times, we can reach out to our guardian angel for answers. Our angel sits on our right shoulder, and even though we may not see it there, it presides over mercy.

Interestingly, we do not keep the same guardian angel throughout our many lifetimes. We have a different one for each incarnation, for each lifetime has its own karma. If we have finished part of what we've come into a lifetime to do and elevate to the next level, then a new angel comes to work with us. Since every angel has its own job, once we've finished a particular correction in our current lifetime, we'll need a fresh angel for the next correction.

A guardian angel is always with us. We are never alone.

Finding Your Guardian Angel

The Creator allows nothing to exist in our lives that cannot be made right one way or another. This is because life is about opportunities and tests calculated to bring us closer to His eternal Light, which is why He grants us the gift of a guardian angel.

Since your guardian angel is unique to you, you will need to undertake your own process to locate that angel. The following exercise can be helpful in getting that process under way. You may find it helpful to record the following instructions and play them back to yourself so that you can keep your eyes closed during the meditation. You can also have someone read these instructions aloud in a slow, measured way as you follow them.

Sit with your feet flat on the ground and your arms uncrossed, allowing energy to flow through your being. (Crossing your arms and legs obstructs this flow of energy.) Lift your eyes slightly above the field of vision (roll your eyes upwards as if towards the top of your head) and close them.

Allow the muscles of your face and your eyes to relax. Now relax the back of your neck, your shoulders, and your hands. Let your arms hang loosely and heavily at your sides. Allow the back of your neck, your spine, and all of your internal organs to relax. Let that warm, easy, relaxed feeling move slowly down your torso to your hips, then down your legs and feet to the very tips of your toes.

Visualize the number three, three times. Then the number two, three times. Then the number one, three times. And now allow yourself some time to do nothing but follow me on this journey in your mind's eye.

Picture yourself climbing a ladder. At the top of the ladder, you can see a beam of Light. You are rising step by step by step, getting nearer and nearer to the Light. You can feel its warmth as you come closer, up the steps.

Now you're standing at the top of the ladder, engulfed in this warm, beautiful, white Light. Embrace it. Feel it soothe your body. Let its warmth flow through you.

Now allow the Light to lead you through a door into a room. Here you find nothing but an easy chair, some cheerful, warm sunlight streaming through a window, and a door that rolls open from the bottom to the top (like a garage door).

Sit yourself down in the chair for a moment and imagine the kind of spiritual entity you would like to be able to call upon when you need it most. Allow yourself to think of that being as devoted to you alone.

Now get up from the chair and go toward the garage-like door. Bend down and start to roll it up, noticing that there is a new source of light behind this door. As you slowly raise the door, envision that being, that spiritual friend with whom you hope to share all your important decisions.

Allow that friend to step out from behind the door and into the room. Embrace this being, for it has waited your entire life for this invitation to become a conscious part of you. Think about what you may want to name it.

If the being hasn't yet materialized, embrace the feeling it gives you. And give it whatever name seems right.

Thank this being for its presence. Draw it close to you. Bless it. Then send it back behind the door.

Now draw the door down from the top. See the light behind it as you pull the door down until the door is closed and the light is gone. You might feel a chill for a moment, but remember that we are never alone. The Creator in His infinite wisdom has ensured the presence of positive forces at all times. And now, even in your darkest moments, you have a new friend to call on. Take comfort in knowing that this first encounter is just the beginning of a lifelong connection that will grow stronger and more comfortable with each passing day.

Now go back to that wonderful easy chair and sit. Relax. Imagining your body going completely limp. And now, while you're still in the chair, feel yourself being lifted up and embraced by the warmth of the Light. Feel it penetrate your being.

Now get up from the chair and start climbing down the ladder.

As you climb down each step, you are slowly re-entering Earthly time. When you're standing at the base of the ladder, take a few deep breaths. Slowly count from one to five: One, two three, four, five.

On the count of five, you may return to the here and now. Welcome back.

Angels bring us the gift of being able to get in touch with the eternal good even in the worst of times. As we develop the consciousness that allows us to use that gift, it gets easier and easier to connect. And we can rest easy, knowing that there will never be a time when our guardian angel won't be there. We can always call on it. Its presence reminds us that no matter how deeply we may fall into darkness, there is always a way out. As long as we draw breath, we're capable of completing our *tikkun*. And thanks to the angels, we're always in the company of friends.

ANGELS OF THE DAY

There are angelic forces at work in our lives that can be called upon to help us in specific circumstances. Scanning the following prayers can activate these forces. Scan the appropriate day's prayer with your eyes, looking from right to left, making a wish as you scan. Meditate on whatever you need help with— overcoming fear, increasing desire, becoming more open—and let the power of the angels come to your aid.

the angels of the day

יוֹם א' יְהוָה

יַוד הֵי וַו הֵי יֵוד הֵי וָאו הֵי

אל שׁדי יאולדרפההייויאוודההיי

אנּא בכוח גדולת ימינך תתיר צרורה

אבְגיתֵץ יְהוָה יְהוָה

סְמְטוֹרייֵה גֵרִיאֵל וְעֵנֵאֵל לְמֵוֵאֵל

ר"ת סגּול

the angels of the day

יוֹם בְּ

MONDAY

יוּד הֵי וָאוּ הֵי יוֹד הֵי וָאוּ הֵי יוֹד הֵי וָאוּ הֵי יוֹד הֵא וָאוּ הֵא

אֵל יהוה יָאוֹלדּפההָאאִיאּוֹודההָאא

קַבֵּל רִנַּת עַמְּךָ שַׂגְּבֵנוּ טַהֲרֵנוּ נוֹרָא

קָרְעֲשָׁטָן יֶהֱוֶה יְהוֹה

שְׁמְעִיאֵל בְּרְכִיאֵל אַהֲנִיאֵל

ר"ת שׂוֹא

the angels of the day

יוֹם גֵּ

TUESDAY

יוֹד הֵא וָאו הֵא יוֹד הֵה וָו הֵה
אל אדֹנָי יאולדֹפההההויווֹדהההה
נֹא גֹבור דורשֹי יוֹזודך כבבֹת שֹמרם
נֹגֹרֹיכש יֵהֹוֹה יֹהוֹה
וזֹיאל להֹדֹיאל מוֹזֹיאל

ר"ת וֹזֹלֹם

◄——— Scanning Direction

the angels of the day

יוֹם דּ׳

WEDNESDAY

יוֹד הָא וָאו הָא יוֹד הֵה וָו הֵה
אֵל אֲדֹנָי יְאוֹלְדָפֶהההֹהֹוִיווֹדֹההֹהֹה
בְּרְכֶם טַהֲרֵם רוֹזֵמִי צִדְקָתֶךָ תָּמִיד גֹּמְלֵם
בַּטְרֶצְתָג יַהֲוֶה יְהוֹה
וֹזֹקִיאֵל רֹהֹטִיאֵל קָדְשִׁיאֵל

ר״ת וֹזַרְק

the angels of the day

יוֹם הֵ

THURSDAY

יְוֹד הֵי וָאו הֵי יְוֹד הֵי וְאו הֵי וְאו הֵי יוֹד הֵי יוֹד הָא וָאו הָא

אל יהוה יאולדפההאאויאוודההאא

חֹסִין קְדִישׁ בְּרוֹב טוֹבְךָ נַהֵל עֲדָתֶךְ

וַקְבְּטַנַע יֱהֹוֶה יֱהֹוֶה

שְׁמוּעֵאל רְעַמִיאֵל קְנִיאֵל

ר"ת שׂוֹרֶק

(הקבוץ מלאכיו בר"ת שׂורק)

← Scanning Direction

the angels of the day

יוֹם וּ

FRIDAY

יוּד הֵי וָו וָו הֵי יוּד הֵי וָאו הֵי

אל שׁדי יאולדרפההייויאוודההיי

יוזיד גאה לעבׂמך פנה זוכרי קׂדושׁתך

יָגְּלֶפָזָק יְהֶוֹהָ יודהוווהו

שׁובמוֹשׁוֹיואולוֹ רופואולוֹ קׂודושׁוֹיואולוֹ

ר"ת שׁרק

the angels of the day

לֵיל שׁבָּת

FRIDAY
SHABBAT EVENING

יוּד הֵי וַאו הֵי

שׁוֹעָתֵנוּ קַבֵּל וּשְׁמַע צַעֲקָתֵנוּ יוֹדֵעַ תַּעֲלוּמוֹת

שְׁקוּצִית יַהֲוָה יְהֹוָה יֵהֶוֶה יֵהוּה

שְׁמְעִיאֵל בְּרָכִיאֵל אַהֲנִיאֵל

ר"ת שׁוא

סְמַטֶוֹרְיָה גַּזְרִיאֵל וְעַנָּאֵל לְבַוָאֵל

ר"ת סְגוֹל

צוּרִיאֵל רַזִיאֵל יוֹפִיאֵל

ר"ת צִירִי

Shabbat has additional energy, so we have three separate angel connections.

← Scanning Direction

the angels of the day

יוֹם שַׁבָּת

SATURDAY
SHABBAT MORNING

יוֹד הֵי וָיו הֵי יוֹד הֵי הֵי וָיו וָיו הֵי

שׁוְעָתֵנוּ קַבֵּל וּשְׁמַע צַעֲקָתֵנוּ יוֹדֵעַ תַּעֲלוּמוֹת

שֶׁקּוְצִית יְהֹוָה יְהֹוָה יְַהֹוָה יְהֹוָה

שְׁמַעְיֵאל בְּרַכְיֵאל אֲהַנְיֵאל

ר"ת שׁוֹא

קַדְמִיאֵל מַלְכִיאֵל צוּרִיאֵל

ר"ת קִמְץ

← Scanning Direction

the angels of the day

מְנֻחַת שַׁבָּת

SATURDAY
SHABBAT AFTERNOON

יוֹד הֵא וָאוֹ הֵא יֵוַד הֵא וָאוֹ הֵא

שַׁוְעָתֵנוּ קַבֵּל וּשְׁמַע צַעֲקָתֵנוּ יוֹדֵעַ תַּעֲלוּמוֹת

שַׁקוֹצִית יֱהֹוִה יֶהֹוָה יֱהֹוַה

שְׁמַעְיֵאל בִּרְכִיאֵל אֲהַנִיאֵל

ר"ת שׁוֹא

פַּדְאֵל תַּלְבַּמִיאֵל (תוּבַמִיאֵל) וַסְדַרְיֵאל

ר"ת פַּתוּז

Tools

Kabbalistic Astrology

You may already have some familiarity with astrology as a means of predicting the future. Newspapers and magazines often carry forecasts of how the day or week or month will go based on our astrological sign: whether it's a good time to start a business, find romance, or make new friends. Conventional astrology, as we know it, is based on the assumption that everything we do is influenced by the heavens. But kabbalistic astrology has an altogether different orientation and purpose. It points out the specific attributes from an earlier lifetime that we have come here to transform. It provides a way for us to become more proactive in our effort to elevate our soul.

As we have seen, our present life is an aggregate of all of our previous lives, during which we faced challenges and made choices. Some of these choices were good and expanded our Desire to Receive for the Sake of Sharing. Those choices promoted our soul's growth. Some choices were not so good and resulted in the growth of our Desire to Receive for the Self Alone. Those choices limited the growth of our soul.

The precise moment we are born is the exact time when our soul is given its best opportunity to become more like the Light. Our karma from previous lives determines which sign we must be born under in order to acquire the traits needed to correct our previous less-than-stellar choices, so that this time around, we can make better decisions and bring our soul closer to the Light.

Kabbalistic astrology provides a roadmap that clearly identifies where we have fallen down in the past and how we might make a correction this time around. Our past choices have determined where we start out in this lifetime, and our present choices will determine where we go next. The individual decisions are ours to make, for the Creator has endowed us with free will.

Our *tikkun* shows us the work we need to do on ourselves in this lifetime. On an astrological chart, our *tikkun* is called the lunar node. This represents the Desire to Receive. The lunar node is made up of two polar opposites: The south node that describes all the baggage we bring into this lifetime, and the north node that describes the path to our correction. Taken together, these nodes are the key to returning to the Light.

THE PRACTICE OF KABBALISTIC ASTROLOGY

To determine which sign represents your *tikkun*, refer to the chart below. The chart is followed by a brief description of your current correction based on your past life. If you would like to learn more about kabbalistic astrology, the Rav has written an excellent book that goes into much greater detail: *Kabbalistic Astrology and the Meaning of Our Lives.*

Tikkun Reference Table

If you were born between these two dates:	Your point of tikkun is:
13 September 1939 to 24 May 1941	Libra
25 May 1941 to 21 November 1942	Virgo
22 November 1942 to 11 May 1944	Leo
12 May 1944 to 13 December 1945	Cancer
14 December 1945 to 2 August 1947	Gemini
3 August 1947 to 26 January 1949	Taurus
27 January 1949 to 26 July 1950	Aries
27 July 1950 to 28 March 1952	Pisces
29 March 1952 to 9 October 1953	Aquarius
10 October 1953 to 2 April 1955	Capricorn
3 April 1955 to 4 October 1956	Sagittarius
5 October 1956 to 16 June 1958	Scorpio
17 June 1958 to 15 December 1959	Libra
16 December 1959 to 10 June 1961	Virgo
11 June 1961 to 23 December 1962	Leo
24 December 1962 to 25 August 1964	Cancer
26 August 1964 to 19 February 1966	Gemini
20 February 1966 to 19 August 1967	Taurus
20 August 1967 to 19 April 1969	Aries
20 April 1969 to 2 November 1970	Pisces
3 November 1970 to 27 April 1972	Aquarius
28 April 1972 to 27 October 1973	Capricorn
28 October 1973 to 10 July 1975	Sagittarius
11 July 1975 to 7 January 1977	Scorpio
8 January 1977 to 5 July 1978	Libra
6 July 1978 to 12 January 1980	Virgo

...to be continued...

If you were born between these two dates:	Your point of tikkun is:
13 January 1980 to 24 September 1981	Leo
25 September 1981 to 16 March 1983	Cancer
17 March 1983 to 11 September 1984	Gemini
12 September 1984 to 6 April 1986	Taurus
7 April 1986 to 2 December 1987	Aries
3 December 1987 to 22 May 1989	Pisces
23 May 1989 to 18 November 1990	Aquarius
19 November 1990 to 1 August 1992	Capricorn
2 August 1992 to 1 February 1994	Sagittarius
2 February 1994 to 31 July 1995	Scorpio
1 August 1995 to 25 January 1997	Libra
26 January 1997 to 20 October 1998	Virgo
21 October 1998 to 9 April 2000	Leo
10 April 2000 to 12 October 2001	Cancer
13 October 2001 to 13 April 2003	Gemini
14 April 2003 to 25 December 2004	Taurus
26 December 2004 to 21 June 2006	Aries
22 June 2006 to 18 December 2007	Pisces
19 December 2007 to 21 August 2009	Aquarius
22 August 2009 to 3 March 2011	Capricorn
4 March 2011 to 29 August 2012	Sagittarius
30 August 2012 to 18 February 2014	Scorpio
19 February 2014 to 11 November 2015	Libra
12 November 2015 to 9 May 2017	Virgo
10 May 2017 to 6 November 2018	Leo
7 November 2018 to 4 May 2020	Cancer
5 May 2020 to 18 January 2022	Gemini

Now that you know which sign represents your *tikkun*, the following information will help you put together the pieces of your puzzle. Because I'm going to focus on the issues you came here to correct in this life, it may seem as if I'm describing your former life as having been overwhelmingly negative. It wasn't. We all have traits to correct; this is just part of the Desire to Receive. Over the course of this lifetime, you may have softened some of these qualities, or you may still have a little work left to do. What I've listed here is the root—the negative quality—that you still may be working on. Please note that for the sake of simplicity, I've described this root in its most potent and extreme form.

If your *Tikkun* (correction) is in Aries . . .

A *tikkun* in Aries tells you that you exhibited the behavior of a Libra in your last life. You were often placed in the role of mediator but had trouble settling conflicts. Taking sides was difficult for you because it meant hurting someone. Rather than make a clear choice, you tried to unite opposing views, and you suffered the consequences of your indecision.

A *tikkun* in Aries points you toward a correction where you must uncover your identity, your unique needs, and your individual desires. **Seek independence and reinforce your self-confidence. This will help you discover your own Light and enable you to become more proactive in all areas of your life.** Along this path of correction, you can stop avoiding conflicts and face each situation as it unfolds, without needing the approval of others.

If your *Tikkun* (correction) is in Taurus . . .

This is one of the most difficult corrections to make because Scorpio was your previous incarnation. At some point in this or a past life, you were the victim of deliberate injustice; possibly you were robbed or driven out of your home. As a result, you are quick to become angry or suspicious. You cling to your possessions when you sense, accurately or not, that someone is about to take them. You would rather sabotage relationships and possessions than have them fall into the hands of others.

Overcome your mistrust and anger to avoid repeating the situations you experienced as a Scorpio. Your *tikkun* directs you toward the positive aspects of Taurus's Light: An appreciation of the beauty and pleasures of this life. This appreciation will let you express yourself without fear of losing your possessions. If you break out of the Scorpio envelope, you can **transform your need for gratification into a true gift of generosity, which will lead you toward a total correction:** *Divine love.* Your newfound peace will appease your soul.

If your *Tikkun* (correction) is in Gemini . . .

You used to have the characteristics of a Sagittarius. You behaved childishly, living from hand to mouth, guided mainly by your own desires and partaking amply of Bread of Shame. Married or in a relationship, you behaved as if you were single. Your thirst for knowledge and study led you to discover new horizons, but you could not commit to any cause that was disconnected from your own interests. Serving others and considering their needs seemed to restrict you.

But Receiving for the Sake of Sharing does not restrain your freedom; it enhances it. By opening yourself to the needs of others in this life, you will overcome the leftover self-absorption that has hindered your ability to elevate to the next level. By communicating openly, you can experience deeper fulfillment and receive the benefit that the Light wants to share with all of us. To do this, **conduct yourself with humility and be respectful of those around you.**

If your *Tikkun* (correction) is in Cancer . . .

You carry pride from your previous incarnation as a Capricorn when you were focused on victory, honor, and respectability. Boosting your reputation and gaining the admiration of others were important to you. You were quick to pass judgment on the mistakes of others. But although you saw yourself as a guardian of the moral order, you failed to practice mercy. As a result, friends fell away. You missed out on the pleasures of life—home, family, friendship—and led an isolated existence in your own secret universe.

Tikkun in Cancer suggests that you relinquish the idea that professional victories, social importance, and your own reputation are the keys to happiness. This is an illusion. Lasting happiness comes from the creation of a warm and loving home. Along your journey, you will discover a world you never knew, a world filled with the wonder, simplicity, and spontaneity of childhood. You will learn flexibility and generosity. **You will elevate your soul and find your way toward the Light lies in the loving eyes of your family and in your dedication and devotion to that love.**

If your *Tikkun* (correction) is in Leo . . .

You carry your former life of an Aquarius into this life. You were considered important and unique in your previous incarnation and have brought inner power, creativity, and ambition into this life. You were not very disciplined, however, and you sought originality at any cost. Because you liked to break the rules, others might not have taken you seriously. Relationships meant the world to you, but you were afraid of being abandoned. You even tolerated abuse in order to maintain closeness, yet you felt you'd given more than you'd received. You let relationships overwhelm you, and because of this, you did not develop your full spiritual potential.

Tikkun in Leo points you toward abandoning your desire for originality in favor of developing your capacity to serve humanity. But pursue this path for yourself, not to win the approval of others. Your ambition will help you find a true and noble cause through which you can share your gifts with humanity. **Your *tikkun* suggests that you will have the opportunity to lead, provided you do so selflessly. As you move toward the Light, use your inner strength, creativity, and originality to reveal new opportunities for sharing.**

If your *Tikkun* (correction) is in Virgo . . .

You had talent in the arts and could have been a famous musician or painter. But like the Piscean you once were, you were preoccupied by your dreams and paid for your emotional reactions. Nourished on sad stories, you had trouble telling right from wrong. You often just let things happen, especially when you were confronted with obstacles, and when things didn't work out, you gave in to misery. Your sensitivity to pain made it difficult, in turn, to relieve that pain, which may have led you to drugs or alcohol. Your intuition may have enabled you to act for others with the intention of helping them, but you couldn't free yourself from your own self-interest. Many of your intended good deeds became excuses for receiving the gratitude of others.

To move toward the Light, you must use more reason and less emotion in making decisions. Self-discipline and determination will keep your feet on the ground and pull you out of dependent relationships. Most of all, stop letting things "happen" to you. Take responsibility for yourself. Learn to speak your mind, both for your own benefit and for the benefit of others. Reflection will be your new tool for tackling problems, but action will put you on the road to your correction. If you succeed in establishing values within yourself and get your head out of the emotional clouds, you will turn your attention toward creating. **Your new motto should be "here and now." This will help you to seize opportunities, overcome obstacles, and make your dreams come true in the real world and thereafter.**

If your *Tikkun* (correction) is in Libra . . .

In your previous life as an Aries, you were self-confident. But your pride led to disappointments, so you wasted energy spinning your wheels. In fact, although you worked hard, you didn't build anything solid. You made a big deal out of failures, became angry, and often dealt rigidly with problems. This brought frustration, which in your present life provokes outbursts that often puzzle those around you. This kind of behavior is damaging, and you have trouble maintaining a long-term relationship.

Tikkun in Libra is one of the more difficult corrections because it means squelching your pride in this life in order to correct the errors of the last one. It points you toward sacrifice in its highest sense. To free yourself from frustration and elevate your soul, devote yourself to a cause beyond yourself. In the past, your ego allowed you only a limited circle of friends, but being part of a larger team will help you regain equilibrium as well as force you to open yourself to what others say. This will soften your personality, and you will become better at mastering your anger. In marriage, you will have a chance to understand real sharing and to gain inner strength from loving someone selflessly. **As you come to understand that the group's success is more important than your own, you will know real happiness. Through selflessness, you can become a righteous person and move toward the Light.**

If your *Tikkun* (correction) is in Scorpio . . .

In your past life, you were Taurus, the Bull. You were in love with beauty and nature, physical pleasure, and the material rather than the spiritual world. However, you were so attached to a certain way of seeing the world that you were reluctant to change. You were possessive and afraid of losing your comfort, so you avoided meaningful experiences. Your life was humdrum. Hemmed in, you neither listened to nor learned much from others.

Abandon the rules that marked your previous life and allow room for spontaneity to enter. This will help you become aware of the illusions that dampened your spirit. Trust the Light to protect you. Initially your comfort and sense of security may feel threatened, but in time, you will become more independent. As long as you consider others in terms of their worth as human beings, your relationships will deepen, especially as you become more capable of empathy. **By letting go of your fears of loss, you can increase your capacity to receive, both spiritually and materially.**

If your *Tikkun* (correction) is in Sagittarius . . .

You have kept the duality that characterized your previous incarnation as a Gemini when you constantly considered your life from two perspectives and thus lived with uncertainty. You had trouble establishing a course of action and sticking to it. This lack of focus hindered your efforts to reach professional success and also slowed your spiritual evolution. To be accepted in a group, you danced to any tune, but that backfired when it led others to see you as a phony.

Your *tikkun* in Sagittarius challenges you to define your aims and accomplish them. Taking on responsibilities provides you with opportunities to establish your own opinions. You can turn your back on your past and confront reality. You bridge this transformation through loyalty. In fact, **you will be so eager for justice that integrity, sincerity, and a refusal to compromise will become central to your progess toward the Light.** You can find your own identity—authenticity will be at the heart of your commitment—and discover your true mission on earth: sharing your wisdom and revealing truth.

If your *Tikkun* (correction) is in Capricorn . . .

Doubts inherited from your previous life as a Cancer can burden you. Having endured the influence of Cancer, you deal with anxiety. Throughout your past life, you managed either to hide your problems or to accept the direction of others. But by doing so, you did not take responsibility. As a consequence, you are a conformist. You may not have opened up to the possibilities of the outside world. Living alone and relying on material goods for your sense of security, you ducked connections with people or ideas. Because of your low self-confidence, you limited your experiences and made yourself stay close to your family, particularly your parents, but then blamed them for your weaknesses.

A correction in Capricorn will teach you maturity. You will cut the umbilical cord with family. You will accept your responsibilities and also look for new ones to dispel your anxieties, thus allowing you to taste the pleasures of risk-taking. You will enjoy committing yourself without forethought. **Identify with a worthy cause, and you will be able to draw on your inner strength to face obstacles. You will gain self-mastery and readiness to fulfill your spiritual mission in life as you elevate your soul and move toward the Light.**

If your *Tikkun* (correction) is in Aquarius . . .

You are a monarch, returning to the physical world to correct the pride remaining from your previous incarnation as a Leo when you lived in the limelight. You loved luxury; as a result, you will now find it hard to do without. At the beginning of your present incarnation, you still sought the admiration to which you were accustomed. You knew how to exploit your power to control your subjects. Your way of expressing a need for love and gratitude was to put yourself at the center of the universe. But living in this artificial world, it was hard for you to find a spiritual path, and overcoming your pride will be difficult, since it was strengthened in previous incarnations.

A *tikkun* in Aquarius can produce roadblocks in your relationships. In marriage, you must abandon your own desires and exchange independence for interdependence. You must recognize that we are all equal. If you let go of honor and glamor, you will succeed in taking control of your personal life and your spiritual evolution. Only then can you know true friendship and universal fraternity and move toward the Light. **You can experience an exceptional adventure in the history of humanity if you manage the most difficult restriction: Silencing your ego and practicing humility while living a simple life.**

If your *Tikkun* (correction) is in Pisces . . .

Your previous life as a Virgo has left you with difficulty detaching from logic. You were absorbed in rationalizations that, although right in the beginning, ultimately became unsatisfying because you saw only the physical side of the picture. Your concern for details turned you into a fussy person. You lost spontaneity, compartmentalizing and labeling according to a set of rules. This Virgo behavior also led to difficulties in your sexual life. Your reluctance to get emotionally involved, coupled with your anxiety about being able to control a relationship, led you to avoid emotional outbursts of any kind. Inflexible in your way of thinking, you had a hard time listening to and learning from others.

A *tikkun* in Pisces suggests that you should not try to perceive the essence of truth through your senses; the Light is the origin of everything physical. Abandoning your need for logical explanations will enable you to erase the doubts that have bothered you. At a more spiritual level, you can experience emotions that will help you change your perception of others, and you will find that by judging them less, they will offer you more. This will kindle within you a love for your fellow-beings and will strengthen your compassion. **Acting in the moment to serve a universal purpose in which you have faith is the key to achieving a true rebirth and attaining universal consciousness.**

Tools

Unveiling the secrets hidden in faces and palms

F ace and palm reading are ancient arts. The Creator gave this knowledge to Adam. From Adam, it passed to Moses, from Moses to King Solomon, and then to Rav Shimon bar Yochai, the author of the *Zohar*. In more recent times, it passed to Rav Isaac Luria (the Ari).

Face and palm reading is not a way to judge or pigeonhole other people. Rather, it's a way to understand our own *tikkun*, our own process, as we work toward returning to the Light. Once we recognize the source of the negative signs from a previous lifetime, we can make a correction, thus elevating our soul to the next level.

The traits listed below show us what we brought from our past lives into this lifetime. Although these traits represent an inborn predisposition, they are not necessarily a reflection of where we currently are. For example, our features could reveal qualities that seem harsh, but we may have overcome them in this life. Abraham Lincoln is a prime example. He had a decidedly frightening, asymmetrical face, but he surmounted all of his flaws in this lifetime and acted for the betterment of mankind. On the other hand, we may have features that depict a gentle nature, which may mean that we have come to this life in order to develop the ability to discern, to make positive judgments, to set boundaries, and to cultivate certain leadership skills.

As you read the lists below, it is important not to judge yourself or others in traditional terms, especially since you're not looking at the whole picture. If anything, these qualities should show us that we cannot judge a book by its cover. For instance, what our society has come to see as unattractive features—a large nose, a gap between teeth, big fleshy ears—are kabbalistic signs of great wealth.

So please use this wisdom wisely. Do not attach a negative connotation to signs like aggressiveness or a positive connotation to signs like kindness. These are simply descriptions. In fact, in some instances, aggressive behavior can be a much-needed trait, while kindness can be a weakness.

Also, each feature needs to be considered as part of the whole. They give us a snapshot of what we came into this life with— the seed level our *tikkun*. Why do we call it "face and palm reading"? Because for a more complete reading, we observe our faces as well as our palms. It is both interesting and cosmically poetic that what is conveyed by our palms always matches what we see in our face, although some traits found in the palm are not expressed in the face and vice versa. For instance, we might see positive elements related to business on our face, whereas we might find negative traits regarding relationships or health on our palms, but we will never find a discrepancy between the two: Our face will never tell us something that will be contradicted by our palms.

Let's look at facial features first. Here are some things to think about when using face reading as a tool. The best time to observe your own face is when you are relaxed. Sadness and anger create their own energy, which distorts perception. Also, strong facial features and lines represent power and might, while less distinct features indicate a loss of energy.

172

FACE READING

Throughout this book, I have discussed how an awareness of reincarnation helps us complete the work our soul came to perform in this world. Important clues about our past incarnations and our *tikkun* can be found in our appearance. Particular lines on our forehead—whether our lips are full or thin; whether our earlobes are fleshy or flat; whether our eyes are close-set or far apart—are all projections of our soul from a previous lifetime. Face reading gives us some tools to recognize the meaning of these signs, which helps us piece together our puzzle. Without the knowledge revealed by our facial characteristics, we may miss great opportunities in this lifetime.

Knowledge of face reading helps us recognize our own flaws. Identifying our flaws helps us to improve ourselves and elevate our soul. For instance, if our features show that we had little self-confidence in our last lifetime, today we'll need to work on developing ways to be more assertive and to behave with greater respect and consideration for our emotional and spiritual well-being. When we do this, we will enjoy a greater capacity to share with others, thus gathering momentum on the path to perfecting our soul.

Hair Texture

- Shiny – Success in the physical domain: Material wealth, leader, politician, well-liked by the community.
- Dull – Less success
- Thick – Has vitality

- Thin – Lack of vitality
- Coarse – Potential to become aggressive
- Kinky – Potential to become angry
  - May have gotten upset quickly
  - Potential to be drawn toward negative actions
  - Judgmental
  - Lacking in decency
  - Leaning toward dishonesty, cruelty, or impulsiveness.
- Wavy/curly – Balanced between being too gentle and too harsh
  - Even disposition
  - Self-confident
  - Balanced and in control as long as you didn't seek only material success

Hair Color (Combine the qualities of hair color with the texture of the hair for a more accurate picture.)

- Red
  - Tendency toward excitability
  - Potential to be fiery if provoked; potential to flare up and fight
  - Could be energetic
  - Active mind: Quick in both thoughts and speech
- Blonde
  - Easily able to become spiritual
  - Quiet, peaceful, stable
  - Practical, direct, to the point
  - Note: Blonde hair softens the more negative traits associated with hair texture and hairline.

- Black or brown
    - Joy in life, excitement, positive energy
    - Fiery energy from within
    - Success in the physical world, but also in the spiritual world if you tried
- White
    - Waning passion of youth: Less drive to win, less of an urge to go crazy from the time you were young
    - More gentleness, softness

Hairline

- Widow's peak (shaped like a heart) – very romantic character
- Baldness in the front (before the age of 30) – a level of dishonesty, lacking integrity, did not walk the talk.
- Bald in the back – tendency toward gossiping
- Note: Kinky, coarse, and/or frizzy hair adds more balance and compassion to any of the above traits. Soft, smooth hair combined with partial baldness adds an aspect of being a crook.

Forehead

- Big, wide, protruding
    - Cleverness, great memory
    - Success in every endeavor
    - Ability to see the bigger picture and see things coming
    - Sensible, indifferent to small details

- Does not come off as being simple or humble
- Round
  - Wise, spiritual
  - Business was not a priority
  - Quick, accomplishes things fast
- Flat
  - Judgmental, lacking tolerance,
  - Vengeful

Forehead Lines: How we behaved in our past lives can appear in the lines on our forehead. Nevertheless, we can be aware of our tendencies and control them. Moses had features that could be seen as negative, but he didn't act upon it. He had three straight lines in his forehead, which means that he controlled his defects.

- Three straight lines – behaved with integrity, honesty
  a) conducted yourself in a decent manner (did not embarrass others or look to put others down)
  b) trusted that there is a bigger picture
  c) put your trust in the Light
- Two straight lines – one of the good qualities of three straight lines is not perfected yet
- One straight line – two of the good qualities of the three straight lines is not perfected yet
- Broken or disconnected line –your actions did not manifest the good features of your face; to reconnect the lines more effort needs to be put into life, allowing the good features (potential) to become manifest

Eyebrows

- Straight – honest, loyal, hard-working, responsible
- Arched – artistic, lover of beauty and art but was perhaps not so practical
- Thick – assertive, authoritarian, controlling
- Thick and wild – unconventional thinker, genius or crazy
- Big space between eyebrows – strong willed, powerful, ability to persevere
- Connected eyebrows – angry, proud, arrogant, intolerant, rude
- White eyebrows – How the trait manifested is dependent on color of head hair.
    - Hair on the head is white, see the description of white hair above.
    - Hair is black or red – there was a disconnect—you appeared to be a kind person but were actually more negative, either a cheat or con man

Eye Position and Shape

- Protruding eyes
    - Adulterer, had the tendency for exaggerated sexual interest and needs to restrict this tendency in this lifetime
    - Arrogant, demanded respect
    - Praised yourself, talked about your accomplishments with pride, shared but only with your own agenda in mind

- Crossed eyes
  - Cheater
  - Presented yourself as a kind, gentle person, although this was not the case, in order to take advantage of others
  - Self-absorbed, selfish
  - Had the evil eye
  - Absorbed energy from others
- Deep-set eyes
  - Cunning, dishonest, a crook especially when dealing with finance and business
  - Hid intentions from others
  - Chased money if not sex
- Close-set eyes
  - Critical and analytical, detail-oriented
  - Pessimistic
  - Stubborn, unwilling to change
- Narrow eyes
  - Closed personality and suspicious
  - Coveted what others had
- Eyelashes
  - Big, thick, and long lashes – sensitive, emotional
  - Thin, short lashes – less sensitive and emotional

Eye Color

- Green
  - Happy and full of joy
  - Always thinking
  - Virtuous and compassionate with strong friendships

- Had wealth and status
- Very successful spiritually
- Blue/grey (clear and bright eyes)
  - Had grace, compassion, a sharing nature
  - Spiritual
- Sparkling black or brown
  - Happy, generous, loving, warm, and kind
- Dark and threatening black or brown
  - Negative: Possessed the evil eye, prone to jealousy
  - Could cause people to get sick
  - Took without giving
- Red/bloodshot/veins in the corners
  - If not for medical reasons could have been a murderer
  - If spiritual, a surgeon
  - Adulterer, obsessed with sex
- White below the iris, above the lower eyelashes
  - Restless
  - Untrustworthy
  - Took advantage of others with no sense of remorse
- Yellow in the whites of the eyes
  - Arrogant and egotistical
  - Sought to enhance a feeling of self-importance
  - Spoke nonsense
- White visible all around the iris
  - Demonstrated a sharing nature
  - Showed compassion and mercy.

Ears: Size and Shape

- Small
    - Very wise and clever, a quick study
    - Successful
    - Very willing to listen, compassionate
    - Always saw the positive in people and situations
    - Success depended on whether you were willing to listen to others, instead of relying on your own smarts.
- Large
    - Slow learner with a steep learning curve
    - Tended to consult and listen to others
    - Didn't see yourself as smart
    - Good at business and politics
    - Spiritual
- Earlobe
    - Fleshy and hanging away from the cheek
        - Purposeful, well-managed life
        - Intellectual
        - Leadership ability
        - Formal and business-like in character as opposed to artistic
    - Small
        - Briefly successful
        - Didn't know how to hold on to money
    - Inner part of the ear protruding
        - Adventurous, daring, led a colorful life
        - Loved to talk and express yourself
        - Did things differently to others
        - Did things your own way

Nose Shape

- Long and sharp, pointy
    - Did not trust anyone, prone to jealousy
    - Unsure about life, which is why you were nosey and looked into the lives of others, busybody
    - Coveted other people's things
    - Conservative, dull, unfashionable
    - Impatient with weakness in others
- Big and fleshy
    - Greedy, ambitious, dissatisfied with less
    - Talent for making money, entrepreneurial, good feel for potential business opportunities
    - Note: If only the tip of the nose is round and fleshy, success came later in life (between the ages of 45 and 52)
    - Diplomat, military leader
- Hooked
    - Shared the big and fleshy nose traits, but modified by a tendency to be more spiritual.
- Crooked
    - Tendency to be dishonest. You found many ways to cheat through speech and behavior, and your cheating wasn't restricted to only business dealings.

Chin Position and Shape

- Protruding, square, or big
    - Great vitality
    - Strong-willed, decisive
    - Persevered when others became tired

- Authoritative, responsible leader
- Receding
  - Lacked self-confidence
  - Weak character
  - Needed support and constant encouragement
- Sharp and pointy
  - Complainer

Mouth

- Narrow (smaller than the width of the eyes)
  - Critical, reserved, cautious
  - Did not like to talk, introverted, prone to be a lone wolf
  - Did not trust others or like company
- Wide
  - Open and cordial
  - Loved people and company
  - Generous, looked to share, helpful
  - Talked a lot

Lips

- Thick
  - Told lies, badmouthed people; gossiped
  - Immodest
  - Insolent and disrespectful
- Thin
  - Cruel and insensitive

- Withered and wrinkled
  - Tended toward evil speech
  - Angry, bad tempered
  - Buffoon
  - Know-it-all
- Luscious lips
  - Sweet, gentle, loving
  - Sympathetic, appreciative, considerate, thoughtful, caring
  - (If a man) Remained single or else married late so that you could bring wealth or a house to the marriage
  - (If a woman) Loyal, soft-spoken, warm, nurturing; married early; wanted to be a mother; cultured and creative.
- Protruding lower lip
  - Demanded acknowledgment for the sake of ego
  - Uncompromising, confrontational, competitive
  - Brutal, cruel, heartless
- Protruding upper lip
  - Sensitive and gentle
  - Loyal

Shape of Face

- Round with a round chin, big eyes, small mouth, fleshy lips
  - Friendly, sympathetic, liked to laugh
  - Procrastinated, looked for easy money and an easy life, did not want to work hard

- Had addictive habits, liked the familiar
- Dependent, lacked self-confidence and personality, high maintenance
- Untrustworthy
- Square with a protruding chin, thick eyebrows, straight nose, high cheekbones
  - Decisive, persevering, patient, stable, practical
  - Stubborn, closed-minded, fixed and limited in your thinking
  - Possibly aggressive, impulsive, and cruel
- Triangular with a pointy chin, wide forehead
  - Intellectual, cerebral
  - Convincing and persuasive, smooth talker, a good salesperson
  - Friendly but non-committal
- Rectangular with a wide and high forehead, arched eyebrows, big clear eyes, big nose, ears close to head, soft, smooth and delicate skin
  - Honest, moral, conscientious
  - Energetic
  - Idealistic, optimistic
  - Practiced what you preached
- Oval: Appearance like a stretched egg
  - Kind, sensitive, tactful, patient
  - Romantic
  - Took a positive approach to life
  - Diplomat, great negotiator
- Pyramidal: Opposite of a triangular face with a narrow forehead, wide jaw, big protruding ears, thick wavy hair
  - Aggressive, angry, disloyal, violent

- Easily lost control, impatient
- Arrogant
- Immoral
- Athletic
- Short neck, short nose
  - Negative and angry
  - Stubborn
  - Lacking in compassion

Color of the Complexion

- Yellow or sickly white (not from illness) with sunken cheeks
  - Unfriendly, loner, bitter
  - Conservative about money
  - Possibly moody or depressed
- Red
  - Energetic, excited, active
  - Ability to inspire and excite others

PALM READING

Palmistry or *hast rekha* can trace its roots back to ancient Greece. Aristotle, a student of Plato, who was thought to have studied Kabbalah, stated that "Lines are not written into the human hand without reason. They emanate from heavenly influences and man's own individuality." (*De Caelo*—On the Heavens)

Aristotle, Hippocrates, and Alexander the Great popularized the laws and practice of palmistry.

Reading palms involves evaluating the hand as a whole as well as the individual fingers, nails, and lines in the hand.

Hands: Flexibility

- Stiff or hard hands: difficult to open and close/inflexible
  - Saw things only your way
  - Closed emotionally and intellectually, resistant to change and new ideas
  - Taciturn and unfriendly
  - Enjoyed working
- Soft, tender, flexible hands
  - Into being natural (no makeup, no fancy shoes or clothes, etc.)
  - Lived in your imagination
  - Loved the easy life and nice things, but unwilling to work for them
  - Talked a lot, did very little
  - Very flexible, easily adaptable

Fingers: Together with other aspects of the hand, the fingers are indicators of the direction of your destiny. Characteristics to consider: finger length, where they touch and meet in relation to the other fingers.

Average Length of Fingers

- Length (relative to the size of the palm)

Short Fingers

- Short fingers
    - Practical, good at details, organized
    - Loved physicality
    - Hard worker, loved to work, full of stamina
    - Quick thinker, impulsive, tended to jump to conclusions
    - A little insensitive

Long Fingers

- Long fingers
  - Lived in an imaginary world of your own
  - Needed encouragement and support all the time

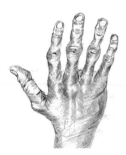

Prominent Knuckles

- Knuckles – protruding joints
  - Loved details, very precise, meticulous, logical
  - Strict
  - Examined and investigated things
  - Monotonous and boring

The Thumb: Most dominant of the fingers

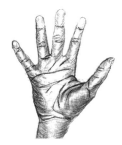

Long Thumb

- Big and long
  - Leadership ability
  - Ability to see the bigger picture

Short Thumb

- Small and short
  - Weak character, doormat-consciousness
  - Lacked passion
  - Didn't take risks

- Degree of stiffness
  - Thumb is stiff, does not bend straight back: Stubborn, strong-willed, mistrustful, opinionated, judgmental
  - Thumb is too flexible (bends all the way back): Lack of self-worth, insipid personality, low self-esteem
  - Thumb bends back but not all the way: Flexible, well-adjusted, able to balance between extremes

Index Finger: Represents and reflects ego, sense of self-worth, leadership ability

Long Index Finger   **Short Index Finger**

- Long (the tip of the finger extends above the halfway point of the middle finger beyond the crease): You were a leader.
- Very long (finger extends beyond or is almost the same length as the middle finger): You might have been a control freak.
- Short (aligned to the middle finger below the halfway mark): You had low self-confidence, tended to be a follower, and had greater difficulty than usual enhancing yourself

Long Middle Finger   **Short Middle Finger**

Middle Finger: Relates to the idea of hard work. When other aspects of the palm, such as lines and mounds connect to this finger it indicates that hard work was key to your destiny. It is your karma that whatever you receive in this life will come from hard work, not luck.

Long Ring Finger   **Short Ring Finger**

Ring Finger: Signifies artistic ability, creativity. Artistic talents (poetry, music, fine arts) are gifts from a past life. If you were inclined toward engineering, you might have become an architect. A ring finger (long and the tip is above the halfway point of the middle finger) indicates that you were more artistic in your past life. If it is shorter, you were less creative.

...to be continued...

Long Pinky Finger   **Short Pinky Finger**

Pinky Finger: Indicator of communicativeness and relationships. Most tips of the pinkies touch on the crease of the ring finger. If the pinky ends above this line, you were more open and communicative; if it ends below, you were more reticent and less communicative.

Nails: Indicate the quality of your health in your past life—and whether or not you were naturally more inclined toward being healthy. Vitality comes with you from a past life. If you did something meritorious in a past life, you do not need to suffer from poor health in this lifetime.

- Color
    - Smooth and pink: Balance and good health
    - Blue: Poor blood circulation
    - Yellow: Possible liver problem
    - Any strange coloration: Predisposition to health problems related to the liver or spleen
- White dots indicate that something good is going to happen or something negative will be averted. It takes about two months for the dot to travel up to the tip of the nail. When the dot reaches that point, the good news will manifest just before the nail is cut.

- Dot on a fingernail of the right hand: You will receive good news that relates to the significance of the finger itself. For example, a white dot appearing on the pinky finger of the right hand could mean that you will hear good news in the area of relationships (perhaps a new relationship is developing).
- Dot on a fingernail of the left hand: You will receive good news related to being protected or saved from something bad. For instance, you could receive a clean bill of health after being tested for a disease.
- Ridges reveal some health problems specifically related to digestion or inner organs.

Mounds: The mounds at the base of the fingers can be big or small; soft or hard. The appearance of the mound determines the strength of the trait governed by the finger the mound is associated with. For example the bigger the mound, the stronger the character, personality, creativity, or sensitivity.

- Harder, bigger, higher mounds intensify the attributes of the finger they are below, rendering the attributes more powerful and effective.

Flat Palm

- Small (flat) soft mounds, on the other hand, show that you had good intentions but did not manifest them; you stayed in a potential state.

Big Mound Below the Thumb

- The mound below the thumb connects to sexuality, sensuality, and warmth.

Characteristics of the Lines on Your Palm: The appearance of the lines indicates their effectiveness.

- Deeper, sharper, clearer lines indicate that a trait existed with more intensity. One clear solid line means the quality of that characteristic was strong during your past life.

- Shallower or broken lines that appear as a chain or hairlines (being made up of many little lines or smaller crosshatches) show these traits were less intense in you.

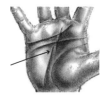

Broken Career Line

- If the line is broken, creating a space between the break and the continuation of the line, it means that something bad happened at that point in your previous incarnation.

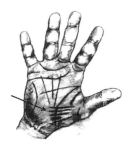

Breaks in the Life Line

- If there is a break—not overlapping but the line crosses another line—it means you experienced turmoil and blockages in this area of your life.

The Four Major Lines

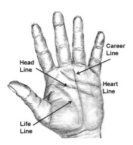

The Four Major Lines

- The *life line* begins between the base of the thumb and the index finger and skirts the thumb mound revealing the length of your former life, events that occurred, your health situation, and your vitality.
  - A shorter line that ends half way down the palm does not indicate that you died young in your last incarnation unless all the other lines stop, too. However, it shows that in this life you may be predisposed to having health problems. Do not take risks or exhaust yourself.
  - Broken lines that appear as a chain or hairlines at the beginning of the life line indicate you had a difficult beginning in life or went through a rough childhood.

- The *head line* begins on the side of the palm between the base of thumb and index finger and usually sits above the start of the life line. The head line crosses the palm toward the pinky finger. It does not reflect intellect. Rather, it indicates clarity, focus, concentration, and ability to think things through without distraction.

Average Head Line

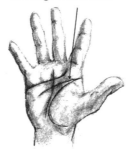

- A strong, well-defined head line shows that you had the capacity for sharp, clear thinking.
- A weak or broken line indicates unclear thinking and confusion.

- The *career line* begins at the base of the palm (sometimes in the center, sometimes not) at the wrist and goes up toward the fingers. The beginning and end of the career line can vary. This line reveals the quality of your career in your past life—whether it came smoothly and with ease or was it difficult and filled with challenges.

Career Line

- The point at which the career line is sharp, clear, and deep is where your career was at its high point.
- Where the career line is weak, unclear, and shallow, you experienced difficulties in your career.
- If the line begins at the base closer to the thumb mound, it means you received assistance in your career from a teacher or mentor.
- If the career line intersects the life line, this indicates that someone showed you the way.
- If the line begins at the wrist, closer to the pinky side of the palm, it means that your career was based on your own creativity and invention.

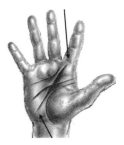

Career Line ending at the Index Finger

- If the line begins in the middle of the palm in line with the index finger, your career was based on hard work.

- The finger that the end of the career line points to shows how your career developed.
- Not having a career line does not mean that you did not have a career. It simply means your career did not come naturally or by fate. You needed to work harder at it than others.

- The *heart line* begins under the pinky mound and travels horizontally across the palm toward the index finger mound, running roughly parallel to and on top of the head line. This line shows how you operated emotionally. It reveals your feelings about love, how you loved, and the physical condition of your heart.

  - A strong line means you knew what you wanted emotionally. If it is a well-defined with no breaks, you were clear about how much to give and how much to take.

Weak Heart Line

  - If the line is less clear, you were more confused about your boundaries and balance from the point of view of your emotions and your giving.
  - If the line is split in two, you had mixed feelings.

Heart Line Ending Between Index and Middle Fingers

- If the line ends between the index and middle finger, it shows that you married for love but also made sure that your feet remained firmly on the ground and you did not lose your head.
- If the line goes all the way up to the index finger, your relationship was connected to leadership.

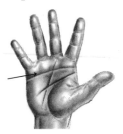

Long Heart Line

- If the line goes from one end of the palm to the other, ending under the index finger, this indicates that you shared too much—so much so that you buried your own needs. You may have lacked self-confidence or a sense of self-worth. You did not protect your own Light as you should have and may have let others take advantage of you.

Short Heart Line

- A shorter heart line (one that doesn't cross half the palm but ends "early") indicates that you tended to be self-absorbed.
- If the line drops down and touches or cuts the head line and the life line, you had a tendency to be dependent. You had few thoughts of your own and felt what others told you to feel.

Conclusion

to be continued...

The *Zohar* says:

In the case of a completely righteous man, all his merits are Above and his transgressions Below. For a completely evil man his transgressions are Above and all his merits are down Below.

—The *Zohar, Behar* 11:67

What does this mean?

We are all a little negative and a little positive. A person who is mostly negative but takes some positive action receives rewards in the physical world now, but his debts follow him into his next lifetime. This way, he will have a chance to correct them. A mostly positive person who takes some negative actions pays his debts in this lifetime. He takes his good credit with him into the next life.

How do we know that our soul is complete and ready to rejoin the Light? When our soul can look back and say, "I had a job to do in this world. I've created a space where there is life, where I've helped others. The people around me have benefitted from my being here. I'm satisfied with myself. I'm satisfied with the things I've done in my life. I feel fulfilled: I have loved, and I am loved."

Being complete means that people know us, and have become better because we existed. We can evaluate what we have accomplished in terms of family, friends, community, or service of some kind. As members of the human race, we feel that there is no place we need to go; we've done all we could. We can remember our lives and fill our ledger with our accomplishments.

However, even in a case like this where we have changed people's lives for the better, we may still come back one more time because we have a higher role to achieve. Or we may have actually done our job, but may decide to come back simply to help others.

Another way to know that a soul is complete is that it no longer fears death. Rav Isaac Luria was only 38 years old when he left this world, but he accomplished a tremendous amount in that short period of time, whereas some people who live to be 100 accomplish very little. Completion of the soul has nothing to do with age. It has to do with being part of something bigger than ourselves.

Once there were two caterpillars who were great friends. They did everything together and loved each other very much. One day, one of the caterpillars disappeared. The other one looked for him everywhere but couldn't find him, so he started to cry. While he was crying, a beautiful butterfly flew over to him. The butterfly asked, "Why are you crying, my dear friend? I am right here."

Until that moment, the sorrowful caterpillar couldn't see the bigger picture. He thought he'd lost his friend, but in truth, he hadn't.

The soul is like a wheel. In order for it to make the most of its energy, it needs to go through its full cycle, the ups and the downs. That journey encompasses many lifetimes. We go from story to story. In one life, we can be rich, and in another, poor. The things we missed in our last life we can do now. The internal force of our soul constantly moves us forward. Even if we are negative and hurtful, eventually the spark of Light that the Creator has given us will return to its source.

Many of us fear the movement of the soul from one life to the next. Perhaps this is because the loved ones who have left us don't come back to assure us that they are fine on the other side. Perhaps we fear death because our soul knows it has not finished what it came to do. But once we realize that death is not the end of the game but just a chance to play part of it over again, we have nothing to fear. In fact, we can be empowered by the understanding that, just as death is not fatal, neither is any action we can take in our past, present, or future lives. Every moment is a moment when we can choose to correct the spark that is our soul so that we can return it to our Creator as perfect as the day it was given to us.

Footnotes:

1. Ian Stevenson, *Children Who Remember Previous Lives: A Question of Reincarnation, North Carolina, USA, McFarland &Company, Inc. Publishers, 2000*

2. Ian Stevenson, *Reincarnation and Biology: A Contribution to the Etiology of Birthmarks and Birth Defects Volume 1: Birthmarks, Praeger Publishers, April 30, 1997*

3. Jeffrey J. Keene, *Someone Else's Yesterday: The Confederate General and Connecticut Yankee: Past Life Revealed, Blue Dolphin Publishing, Inc., Nevada, USA, 2003, page 2.* Photographs reprinted with express permission of Jeffrey Keene.

4. *ABC NEWS, Primetime,* American Broadcasting Company, April 15, 2004, 06:48PM, Television.

5. Barbro Karlen, *And the Wolves Howled: Fragments of Two Lifetimes, Clairview Books, London, 2000, pages 5 & 6.*

Wisdom From Karen Berg

God Wears Lipstick
By Karen Berg

This groundbreaking and bestselling book reveals the power that's innate to every woman. From a Kabbalalistic perspective, Karen Berg outlines life's deeper meaning, and gives tangibles solutions to issues women face today. She delves into the spiritual purpose of relationships—to reach our highest potential—and the way to enrich our connection to our self, our mate, our children, and God.

Simple Light
By Karen Berg

This book delivers a message that is simple, direct, and straight from the heart: Light, the source of all joy, comes from unconditional love and sharing. A collection of insights culled from Karen Berg's writings and teachings over the last 30 years, the wise words shared here are both personal and universal. Whether talking about family, relationships, work, faith, life or death, Karen always manages to keep it real while finding Light in the ordinary as well as the mysterious. *Simple Light* is not intended to be read in one sitting or sequentially, although it can be. It's food for moments of thought and inspiration.

More Ways to Bring the Wisdom of Kabbalah into your Life

Wheels of a Soul
By Rav Berg

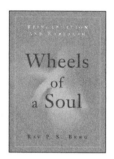

In *Wheels of a Soul*, Kabbalist Rav Berg explains why we must acknowledge and explore the lives we have already lived in order to understand the life we are living today. Make no mistake: You have been here before. Just as science is now beginning to recognize that time and space may be nothing but illusions, Rav Berg shows why death itself is the greatest illusion of all.

Immortality: The Inevitability of Eternal Life
By Rav Berg

Rav Berg offers penetrating insights into the age-old mysteries of life, death, and immortality. He explores the true meaning of "mind over matter," and reveals why our own consciousness holds the keys to unending life. By opening ourselves to spiritual challenges we can defeat "death" once and for all. This new and revised edition draws upon the Rav's personal story and brings that story up to date.

The Power of Kabbalah
By Yehuda Berg

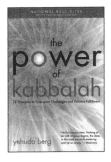

The familiar reality is the physical 1 percent material realm in which we live, yet there is another dimension—the world beyond our five senses. According to Kabbalah, this is called the 99 percent realm. Everything we truly desire: love, joy, peace of mind, freedom, is available when we connect to the 99 percent reality. The problem is that most of us have inadvertently disconnected ourselves from this dimension. Imagine if we could access this source at will, and on a continuing basis. This is the power of Kabbalah. This foundational text features new content and is more accessible for meeting today's current challenges. Use the exercises included to break free of prevalent beliefs and habits which lead to negativity. Readers will discover how to align their actions with their higher purpose, and become conscious of the unlimited possibilities in their own life.

Angel Intelligence
By Yehuda Berg

Angels facilitate the circulation of energy throughout the non-physical universe. Invisible, intangible, and yet they influence us; angels serve as the infrastructure of the spiritual world. Some have existed forever—archangels, angels of the days of the week and of the zodiac, guardian angels, and the Angel of Death. But other angels are created by our actions—good or bad. When we are mindful of our actions, we are able to harness the power of angels, transform ourselves, and find greater fulfillment.

Secrets of the Zohar: Stories and Meditations to Awaken the Heart
By Michael Berg

The *Zohar*'s secrets are the secrets of the Bible, passed on as oral tradition and then recorded as a sacred text that remained hidden for thousands of years. They have never been revealed quite as they are here in these pages, which decipher the codes behind the best stories of the ancient sages and offer a special meditation for each one. Entire portions of the *Zohar* are presented, with the Aramaic and its English translation in side-by-side columns. This allows you to scan and to read aloud so that you can draw on the *Zohar*'s full energy and achieve spiritual transformation. Open this book and open your heart to the Light of the *Zohar*!

Secrets of the Bible
By Michael Berg

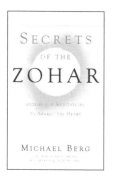

The *Secret of the Bible* is a lifelong pursuit and there are many teachings within its veiled text. Bringing forward a fresh and relevant message about our purpose, and how to make life better, kabbalistic scholar, Michael Berg, imparts wisdom from decades of research and sources unique to his lineage. Gems of insight from the *Zohar*, Rav Berg, Rav Ashlag, Rav Isaac Luria (the Ari) as well as other known kabbalists are complemented by lessons from the ages. Kabbalists believe that the Bible is not just a book of stories or an historical archive of events: It is a guide to understanding the nature of this world, of life, and of the planet. Although these events physically took place thousands of years ago, there are transcendent fundamentals hidden within each tale. Michael drills through complex concepts to reveal essential truths. He utilizes biblical texts to expand our perception to see God in everything and everyone. Although Michael shares ideas that can awaken a desire for transformation, the gift he offers is another view of the Bible and its secrets.

The *Zohar*

Composed more than 2,000 years ago, the 23-volume *Zohar* is a commentary on biblical and spiritual matters written in the form of conversations among teachers. It was given to all humankind by the Creator to bring us protection, to connect us with the Creator's Light, and ultimately to fulfill our birthright of transformation. The *Zohar* is an effective tool for achieving our purpose in life.

More than eighty years ago, when The Kabbalah Centre was founded, the *Zohar* had virtually disappeared from the world. Today, all this has changed. Through the editorial efforts of Michael Berg, the *Zohar* is available in the original Aramaic language and for the first time in English with commentary.

We teach Kabbalah, not as a scholarly study but as a way of creating a better life and a better world.

Who We Are:

The Kabbalah Centre is a non-profit organization leading the way in making Kabbalah understandable and relevant in everyday life. The Centre was founded by Rav Yehuda Ashlag in 1922, and now spans the globe with brick-and-mortar locations in more than 40 cities as well as an extensive online presence. Our funds are used in the research and development of new methods to make Kabbalah accessible and understandable.

What We Do:

We translate and publish kabbalistic texts, develop courses, classes, online lectures, books, audio products; provide one-on-one instruction, and host local and global energy connections and tours, and provide on-going spiritual services. As the principles of Kabbalah emphasize sharing, we provide a volunteer program so that our students can participate in charitable initiatives.

How We Teach:

For every student, there is a teacher.

Our goal is to ensure that each student is supported in his or her study. Teachers and mentors are part of the educational infrastructure. Many of our classes take place in physical locations around the world; however, with today's increasing need and desire for alternative ways of learning, The Kabbalah Centre also offers instruction by phone, in study groups, and online through Webinars and classes, as well as self-directed study in audio format.

Student Support:

Because Kabbalah can be a deep and constant study, it is helpful to have a teacher on the journey to acquiring wisdom and growth. With more than 300 teachers internationally serving over 100 locations, in 20 languages, there is always a teacher for every student and an answer for every question. All Student Support instructors have studied Kabbalah under the supervision of Kabbalist Rav Berg. For more information call 1 800 Kabbalah.

Kabbalah University (ukabbalah.com):

Kabbalah University (ukabbalah.com) is an online university providing lectures, courses, and events in English and Spanish. This is an important link for students in the United States and around the globe, who want to study Kabbalah but don't have access to a Kabbalah Centre in their community. Kabbalah University offers a library of wisdom spanning 30 years. This virtual Kabbalah Centre presents the same courses and spiritual connections as the physical centers with an added benefit of streaming videos from worldwide events.

Kabbalah Publishing:

Each year, we translate and publish some of the most challenging kabbalistic texts including the *Zohar*, the *Writings of the Ari*, the *Ten Luminous Emanations* and essays from Rav Ashlag. We synthesize this wisdom into beginner and intermediate level books, which are distributed and published in more than 30 languages.

Kabbalah Museum:

We gather and preserve original kabbalistic texts and rare manuscripts that are housed in Los Angeles. We make these texts available online for students and scholars to view. These important texts enable us to continue to lead the way in the education of Kabbalah.

Through the merit of this book may my father

Yichiel Mordechai ben Avraham David's

יחזיאל מרדכי בן אברהם דוד

soul live eternally to guide and protect our family.

To the man who spent his lifetime spreading goodness

in this world, may these sparks of Light last forever

and may we follow in his path that he has lit for

generations to come.

May we have the merit to stay in the consciousness

to see that everything is exactly as it needs to be,

which leads to constant fulfillment, the ultimate way

to live a life of happiness.

That my family will follow the path of the Light

forever with certainty and appreciation.

To awaken the hearts of others to want to take

the road that leads to more Light.

This book is also dedicated to

Michael ben Moshe

מיכאל בן משה

may his soul be immortalized and provide his family

with guidance and peace.

With so much love and appreciation to the Berg family

for bringing this wisdom to us and for making it so

accessible to reach these levels of consciousness on

a daily basis.

Debbie, Jeff, David and Racheli

דבורה, עזרא, דוד ורחל